THOMAS NAST

ЖK

The Artist in Color

By

Christine Hayes

RoseDog❧Books

PITTSBURGH, PENNSYLVANIA 15222

RoseDog Books
701 Smithfield Street
Pittsburgh, PA 15222
Visit our website at *www.rosedogbookstore.com*

ISBN: 978-1-4349-8664-1
eISBN: 978-1-4349-7659-8

Th: Nast.

Sarah Nast

2010 ©
Christine Hayes

Nast

This Book is dedicated to The Memory of

Thomas Nast

To his honour, his courage of conviction, and his steadfast, unrelenting stand against corruption, and his unyielding defense of right.

Disclaimer

My two major sources for the information in this book were my personal copy of Albert Bigelow Paine's 1904 biography of Thomas Nast, and the Library of Congress where I found images with no known restrictions on publication, and historic newspaper articles out of copyright. If any image falls outside these categories, it was re sketched by me and enhanced in PSP X2.

I make no claim to being a history major or even a history buff and came to obvious conclusions based on common sense while addressing Mr. Nast's images. I, like Mr. Nast, am neither Democrat nor Republican; rather, I am an American who simply wants everyone to obey our laws and do what is in the best interest of the nation regardless of personal agenda, just as he did.

Finally, I would like to give all credit to Mr. Nast himself who generously applauded all who used his images to spread the word against corruption, tyranny, and anarchy. It was easy for me to bring his images to life in color, but he is the one who actually reflected life in his images; without his original work, my work would not have been possible.

Christine Hayes
2011

Introduction

This book honors the art of Thomas Nast's sketches; their wonderful detail and thorough theme development through auxiliary vignettes surrounding the central picture, and strives to bring them to life in color.

Mr. Nast was one of the greatest artists who ever lived, yet his strong moral political opinions overshadowed his wonderful and unique abilities to manifest his limitless imagination into hardcopy through caricatures and whimsical fancy, as well as fantastic displays of romantic idealism. Mr. Nast stood for 'right', but politically he was not 'on the right' extreme of either Socialist or Conservative Ideology. In spite of being labeled a Republican by most sources, sources that merely repeated other sources in a cursory manner, the astute observer would identify him as a Moderate Independent who supported those persons who stood for adherence to law and order, and the best interest of the country regardless of which party they represented. Mr. Nast was fiercely patriotic and loyal to America, his adopted country, and he could not abide corruption or lawlessness in any form.

Mr. Nast was an artist of limitless range and illustrated many fairytales as well as his serious and profound renditions of military actions in the Civil War. The original creation of Saint Nicholas resulted from his illustration of the poem, The Night Before Christmas, and expressed his warm memories of Christmas in the small Bavarian town where he was born. He illustrated many children's books and in my opinion, these extravagant displays of his imagination are nothing less than a magnificent wonder. While I can paint, I prefer to draw, and I can attest that it is the most time consuming of artistic expression. Mr. Nast was on a time schedule and had to produce a weekly sketch for publication. It is almost unbelievable that he not only expressed such detail in his drawings, but that he did so in such a short amount of time.

There are thousands of books, magazine articles, and Internet Web sites devoted to Thomas Nast. Every encyclopedia has references about him. The Library of Congress has a body of his work, albeit limited compared to his overall accomplishments. An online search at WorldCat.org for Nast books available through libraries reveals over 600 hits. There is a huge listing of over 750 items of Nast work for sale on E-Bay. A Google search reveals a staggering 300,000 plus websites and a Yahoo image search offers 13,400 hits. And believe it or not, a You-Tube search reveals over 80 videos. All of these venues invariably list the quintessential Thomas Nast biography by Albert Bigelow Paine, 1904, as their primary source, or an alternate source that ultimately derived their information from that primary Nast source, creating a chain of sources referencing each other but originating with Mr. Paine's book. I will acknowledge this is not a research paper; rather an effort to compliment the incomparable talent and courage of a very honorable man. None of the many venues of Nast information I have perused highlight his amazing artistic talent and remarkable insight and humor in expressing that talent; rather, his political views are almost exclusively made the main focus of his extraordinary body of work of over 3,000 sketches. While my main objective is to bring attention to the incredible artistic talent of Mr. Nast, I was so impressed with the political landscape of his time, and how it mirrors our own society in present day America, that I decided to include some of his renditions of national concerns, then as now over a hundred years later. I actually wonder if Mr. Nast could have been clairvoyant for he stood against the ills that plague our present day society, so either he foresaw these circumstances or history is repeating itself. Did the times of 150 years ago really mirror what our nation, and the world is going through now? I will let Mr. Nast's sketches speak for themselves.

Thomas Nast had strong views about everything which he had no qualms about aggressively illustrating through his sketches, in particular his avid hatred of the Confederate South during the Civil War. I have read statements plucked from thin air that he was a liberal, or just as erroneous, that he was a rightwing extremist, and that his father was a socialist who did not agree with the government's control of the area in Germany where they lived and that is why he sent his family to America. These loosely conjectured opinions come from an inaccurate American perspective of what life was like in the area of the world where Mr. Nast was born and spent the first six years of his life. The governing body throughout Europe throughout early history has been one of Socialism, either of Liberal Socialist Communism, or of Conservative Socialist Nationalism such as Hitler and the Third Reich, and from time to time, a union of Church and State, the Holy Roman Empire, of which the First, Second and Third Reich were all about. It is probable that his very strong political views resulted from being born in the German region of Bavaria in the small town of Landau, a few miles north of the French province of Alsace Lorrain whose long history was politically turbulent and insecure. Young Thomas Nast migrated with his family to America when he was six years old to escape the political turmoil. Much of his extensive body of work reflects strong sentiments against big government, political and corporate corruption, and injustice that continue to hound our society over a hundred years after his death in 1902. He also had a close personal relationship with our military and supported strong military readiness. Mr. Nast has no courageous contemporary in today's political commentary with the possible exception of Glenn Beck, and it is intriguing to speculate what he would say about the State of the Union today. Since he obviously had a tremendous sense of humor, I think he might say in exasperation, "Give it to the Confederacy", an entity that he held in great distain.

The voluminous amount of information at ones disposal through thousands of pictures, historic newspaper articles, and genealogy sites provide a look into the personal life of Thomas Nast. My endeavor is purely personal; to spotlight Thomas Nast's remarkable artwork and present it in color, and share some anecdotal bits of information about the man and his family. If Mr. Nast is looking down from some celestial studio, I hope he thinks I did his images, and his family, proud.

Foreword

I was first introduced to Thomas Nast in 2006 during an online search for Civil War images and among the search results was his sketch titled "Christmas Eve". I was struck by the detail and emotional visual impact of this exceptionally beautiful picture. I had just bought a book about a Civil War battle in West Virginia for my son who is a serious Civil War history buff, one of several books I have purchased for him by author Terry Lowry, a West Virginia Civil War historian. This particular book is entitled "Last Sleep, The Battle of Droop Mountain". I had skimmed through the book and read the last chapter about ghosts on the battle site and surrounding area. My son is deaf and I wanted to be able to answer questions if he had any about the book. I was born in West Virginia and our family history is primary to that state so my son was very interested in the limited Civil War events that occurred there. As soon as I saw Thomas Nast's sketch of "Christmas Eve", I immediately thought of the book "Last Sleep" because of the row of graves in the Nast picture. It seemed to me the book titled, "Last Sleep", and the "Christmas Eve" sketch by Thomas Nast, were meant to be together. I have had a close and personal relationship with the memory of Mr. Nast since that day in 2006, and I want to shed a personal light on this area of his life that has, heretofore, not been done.

Acknowledgements

I want to express gratitude for the worldwide online public records at FamilySearch.org from the Church of Jesus Christ of Later Day Saints which is generously free to all searching for their family history, and for their permission to include data from vital records on their Web site.

Also thanks to The Library of Congress where one can find a plethora of artwork in the Public Domain as well as Historic Newspapers in which there is a huge amount of articles about Thomas Nast from 1860 to 1922. I know our tax dollars pay for the privilege to use it but I am thankful that we have such a wonderful service.

I want to express my gratitude to Records of the Redpath Chautauqua Bureau, University of Iowa Libraries, Iowa City, Iowa for permission to use the Thomas Nast Jr. talent brochure from 1901. They were gracious and helpful with a quick response.

I also want to thank Nan Card at the Rutherford B. Hayes Presidential Center for her patience and help in acquiring photos and correspondence, and for granting permission to transcribe family letters as well as articles in Mrs. Nast's handwriting dictated by Mr. Nast. Look for "Courtesy of the Rutherford B. Hayes Presidential Center' in association with the pictures of Edith and Julia Nast 1888, and Mabel and Cyril Nast 1880, as well as transcriptions of several articles and letters.

Special thanks to my cousin and good friend Pat Reed who taught me how to use Paint Shop Pro Photo X2. I did develop a method of hand painting the images in the beginning, but PSP was helpful in improving and polishing my sketches, restoring and painting images from Mr. Paine's book and the Library of Congress, as well as allowing me to make a "tube" of the copyright symbol and Mr. Nast's signature to apply on the illustrations with the click of a mouse. PSP has a steep learning curve and Pat was patient in helping me climb that mountain.

First and foremost, as I've collected information and examples of his work, I allowed my common sense and intuitive nature to guide me in my quest to honor Thomas Nast and clear up some misconceptions about him, his life and his point of view. In that vein, I want to give special thanks to my Mother, Goldie May Boling Stanley, for bringing me up with common sense and a sense of right. I hope she joins Mr. Nast in smiling down on me for my efforts.

And finally to my own precious copy of Albert Bigelow Paine's classic biography of Mr. Nast from which all rivers of information flow and to which all roads lead. My book about Mr. Nast's family and personal life compliments Mr. Paine's book and in no way diminishes his work.

ILLUSTRATIONS

The Political Statements of Thomas Nast

Liberty Is Not Anarchy 1886
Party Whip 1885
Immigrants Apr 1877
Church & State 1875
Change 1880
A Financial Lesson Aug 1876
Ideal Money Jan 1878
Inflation 1876
Always Killing the Goose That Lays the Golden Egg Mar 1878
Our Military 1874
The Irish 1880

THE FAMILY OF THOMAS NAST

Thomas Nast was born 27 Sep 1840 in Landau, a small town just a few miles north of Alsace Lorraine on the French and German border. He came to America with his mother, and by some accounts an older sister named Catherine, in 1846. Other accounts say Catherine was a cousin. I have been unsuccessful in finding Mr. Nast, his mother, or the relative Catherine on the 1850 and 1860 United States Federal censuses; neither have I been successful in finding the Nast family on any immigrant passenger list in 1846 or 1851, the two documented possible years of their travel.

Biographer Albert Paine recites a remembrance by Thomas Nast of fireflies outside their living quarters in Havre, France while waiting for their departure. If Thomas actually did make that voyage in 1846, he came by way of documented ship departures from Havre to New York. Those ships are listed here with some speculation relating to the possible occurrence of firefly activity in the months of departure.

The Louis Philippi arrived 29 Apr 1846 in New York City. Since an arrival date of April would have meant a departure date from Havre in February, this would have been too early for fireflies. The ship's partial list of passengers was from Germany.

Another 1846 ship from Havre to New York was the Globe. Its arrival date was 30 May 1846 and the partial list of passengers was from Germany. This also might have been too early in the year for fireflies considering it took approximately sixty days to make the voyage which would have meant a departure from Havre in March.

The third ship in 1846 was the Shakespeare which arrived in New York on 26 Sep 1846. This may have been the most likely ship if we consider the firefly memory of Mr. Nast. July would definitely be firefly friendly. Another clue would be the passenger list; a mixture of German and French would be representative of the Alsace Lorraine area close to the small town of Landau where Mr. Nast was born and where he lived with his family until age six when they migrated to America.

The fourth voyage that year was the Palestina with a 5 Oct 1846 arrival and a partial passenger list of French.

Fifth was the Meta arriving 19 Nov 1846 with a partial passenger list of German.

The last ship was the Uttica arriving 14 Dec 1846 which would have been far too late to see fireflies in October. If Thomas Nast left Alsace and traveled to Havre, then departed on a ship to New York in 1846, logic says he traveled on the Shakespeare but I have not found a total list of passengers on any of these ships.

There seems to be a discrepancy on the 1900 Federal United States census on which it is recorded that Mr. Nast arrived in America in 1851 and that he had been in America for 49 years. It seems unlikely to me that he would have not known his own year of immigration and the number of years he had lived in the United States, but all other notations in Thomas Nast history lists the 1846 date as the date he came to America. Many times, sources cite other sources that are themselves erroneous. The quintessential authority on Thomas Nast, "TH. NAST His Period and His Pictures", by Albert

Bigelow Paine, 1904, seems to be the source for all other information about Mr. Nast. Mr. Paine discussed the book with Thomas Nast before Mr. Nast's death but I conjecture that since Mr. Nast died in 1902 and Mr. Paine was in the process of writing the book, he probably got some of his data from Widow Sarah and son Cyril after Mr. Nast's death, which may not have been accurate. I must take the only actual documentation of the 1900 census at face value, on which Mr. Nast would have personally given the information since he worked at home, unless and until, a passenger list proves his arrival from Havre to New York City in 1846. An arrival date of 1851 would mean he was eleven years old when he migrated to America. This is just one of the mysteries about Mr. Nast that begs an answer.

It is also of interest that I cannot find Thomas or his mother on the 1850 census as one would expect if he indeed arrived in New York in 1846; however, it was common for people to be missed by the census taker, so not appearing on the 1850 census does not mean he was not in New York at the time. They could not speak English and were probably living in a relative's or friend's apartment in a crowded city tenement. It is also of interest to me that Mr. Paine describes Mr. Nast as leaving Havre on a beautiful American ship; there actually was a ship named Amerika that sailed from Germany to New York on 2 Jan 1851, but of course according to Mr. Paine, the port of departure was Havre and January is not firefly weather. The only ship to sail from Havre to New York in 1851 was the Baltimore on 19 Aug 1851. This could have also been interpreted as an American ship. Thomas Nast's father Joseph arrived in America four years after his family, so he either arrived in 1850 or 1855 depending on the arrival year of his family, and he died a few short years later. I will leave to other researchers with direct access to New York immigration records to determine these dates in contention. If the immigration record of Mr. Nast Sr. could be determined, it would prove the arrival year of the Nast family four years earlier even if no passenger list is found for them.

Thomas Nast Birth:

Thomas Nast Male Christening/Baptism Date 27 Sep 1840 Place Sankt Maria, Landau (Pfalz), Bayern, Germany Birth Date 26 Sep 1840, Birthplace Sankt Maria, Landau (Pfalz), Bayern, Germany, Father's Name *Josephi Thomae Nast*, Mother's Name *Apolloniae Abriss*.

My intent in presenting records is not to diminish Albert Paine's book about Thomas Nast, however, I would be remiss if I did not report what I have found. Mr. Paine describes a regular Sunday afternoon outing to a small cemetery in Landau, Germany by the Nast family to visit the graves of Nast's brothers. This was in actuality two sisters and a brother.

The older deceased brother of Thomas Nast:

Joannes Paulus Nast Male Baptism/Christening Date 11 Oct 1838 Place Sankt Maria, Landau (Pfalz), Bayern, Germany, Birth Date 09 Oct 1838 Place Sankt Maria, Landau (Pfalz), Bayern, Germany, Death Date 15 Aug 1839, Father's Name *Josephi Thomae Nast*, Mother's Name *Apolloniae Abriss*.

An older deceased sister of Thomas Nast:

Anna Nast Female Baptism/Christening Date 04 Jun 1834 Place Sankt Maria Katholisch, Landau in Pfalz Stadt, Pfalz, Bavaria, Death Date 02 Jan 1839, Father's Name *Thomae Nast*, Mother's Name *Appolloniae Abriss*

An older deceased sister of Thomas Nast:

Carolina Nast Female Baptism/Christening Date 16 Jun 1836 Place Sankt Maria Katholisch, Landau in Pfalz Stadt, Pfalz, Bavaria, Death Date 07 Oct 1838, Father's Name *Thomae Nast*, Mother's Name *Apolloniae Abriss*.

Thomas Nast's parent's marriage record: *Josepham Thomam Nast* and *Apolloniam Abriss* 21 Aug 1834 Sankt Maria Katholisch, Landau In Pfalz Stadt, Pfalz, Bavaria. Groom's parents: *Pauli Nast* and *Catharina Walbrunn*; Bride's parents: *Christophori Abriss* and *Catharinae Vogt*.

Appolonia Abris b. 10 Feb 1801 Offenbach, Bayern, Germany, Offenbach, Pfalz, Bavaria Father's name: *Christophoro Abris*, Mother's name: *Eva Catharina Vogtin*

Apollonia Abriss Nast's older sister: *Eva Elisabetha Abriss* b. 22 Apr 1798 Offenbach, Bayern, Germany, Offenbach, Pfalz, Bavaria, Father's name: *Christophori Abriss*, Mother's name: *Catharinae Vogt*.

Elizabeth's child: *Catharina Abriss* b. 20 May 1838 ROEMISCH-KATHOLISCHE, RAMBERG, PFALZ, BAVARIA, Mother's name: *Elisabethae Abriss*

In my opinion, Apollonia Abris Nast's sister Elizabeth Abriss's child Catherine, or her brother Michael's daughter Catharina are the most likely candidates to be the relative that accompanied their aunt Apollonia Nast and their cousin Thomas to America. Elizabeth was unmarried and the homeland was in political turmoil so it would have been reasonable that she would have enjoined her sister Apollonia to take her little daughter with her to a better future in America. But, whichever Catherine Abris came to America with Mrs. Nast and her son Thomas in 1846, the other Catherine came to America in 1859 on the ship Mercury.

Apollonia Abriss Nast's younger sister: *Catharina Abris* b. 25 Mar 1807 Offenbach, Bayern, Germany, Offenbach, Pfalz, Bavaria, Father's name: *Christophoro Abris*, Mother's name: *Catharina Vogt*.

A younger brother of Apollonia Abriss Nast: *Michaelis Abris* b. 5 Aug 1803 Offenbach, Bayern, Germany, Offenbach, Pfalz, Bavaria, Father's name: *Christophoro Abris*, Mother's name: *Eva Catharina Vogtin*.

Michael's marriage: *Michaelem Abriss* and *Catharinam Doppler* 07 Jan 1832 Mörlheim, Offenbach, Bayern, Germany, Groom's parents: *Christophori Abriss* and *Catharinae Vogt*; Bride's parents: *Georgii Michaelis Doppler* and *Margarethae Horter*.

Michael's children: *Heinricus Abriss* 07 May 1834 Offenbach Am Queich, Pfalz, Bavaria, Bayern, Germany, Parents: *Michaelis Abriss* and *Catharinae Dobler*

Catharina Abriss 11 Oct 1837 Katholisch, Offenbach Am Queich, Pfalz, Bavaria, Bayern, Germany, Parents: *Michaelis Abriss* and *Catharinae Doppler*.

Barbara Abriss 23 Jan 1839 Katholisch, Offenbach Am Queich, Pfalz, Bavaria, Bayern, Germany, Parents: *Michaelis Abriss* and *Catharinae Doppler*.

Maria Catharina Abriss 07 Jul 1841 Offenbach Am Queich, Pfalz, Bavaria, Bayern, Germany, Parents: *Michaelis Abriss* and *Catharinae Doppler*.

Margretha Abriss 12 Dec 1843 Katholisch, Offenbach Am Queich, Pfalz, Bavaria, Bayern, Germany, Parents: *Michaelis Abriss* and *Catharinae Doppler*.

Maria Katharina Abriss 29 Jun 1848, Christening: Katholisch, Offenbach Am Queich, Pfalz, Bavaria, Parents: *Michaelis Abriss* and *Catharinae Doppler*.

Apollonia Abriss Nast's mother: *Eva Catharina Vogt* b. 27 Nov 1761 EVANGELISCHE, MUSSBACH, PFALZ, BAVARIA, Bayern, Germany, Father's name: *Frank Christoph Vogt*, Mother's name: *Elisabetha*.

Apollonia Abriss Nast's father: *Josephus Christophorus Abris* 27 Sep 1760 Offenbach, Bayern, Germany, Pfalz, Bavaria, Father: *Joanne Georgio Michaele Abris*, Mother: *Maria Catharina Buschin*.

Apollonia Abriss Nast's parents marriage: *Christophorum Abris* and *Catharinam Vogt* 15 NOV 1790 Katholisch, Klingenmuenster, Pfalz, Bayern

Christopher Abriss's older sister, the aunt of Apollonia Abriss Nast: *Catharina Barbara Josepha Abris* 06 Feb 1757 Birth Place: Offenbach, Pfalz, Bavaris, Christening: Offenbach, Bayern, Germany, Father: *Joanne Georgio Michaele Abris*, Mother: *Maria Catharina Buschin*.

Christopher Abriss's younger brother, the uncle of Apollonia Abriss Nast: *Joannes Ignatius Engelhardus Josephus Abris* b. 22 Jun 1763 Offenbach, Pfalz, Bavaria, Christening: 23 Jun 1763 Offenbach, Bayern, Germany, Father: *Joanne Georgio Michaele Abris*, Mother: *Maria Catharina Buschin*.

The parents of Apollonia Abriss Nast's grandfather *Joanne Georgio Michaele Abris's*, birth: *Georgius Michael Abris* b. 22 May 1729, Christened: Katholisch, Kandel, Pfalz, Bavaria Father: *Joannis Georgii Abris*, Mother: *Catharinae*

Apollonia Abriss Nast's grandparent's marriage: _Joannem Georgium Michaelem Abris_ and _Mariam Catharinam Busch_ 27 Jun 1752 Offenbach, Bayern, Germany, Groom's parents: _Georgii Abris_ and _Annae Catharinae Rapp_, Bride's parents: _Andreae Busch_ and _Catharinae Garrecht._

Apollonia Abriss Nast's grandmother's birth: _Maria Catharina Busch_ b. 26 Feb 1723 Offenbach An Der Queich, Pfalz, Bayem, Parents: _Andreas Busch_ and _Eva Catharina Gerachin_.

Apollonia Abriss Nast's great grandparents marriage: _Andreas Busch and Eva Catharina Gerachin_ 4 May 1722 Offenbach, Bayern, Germany, Pfalz, Bavaria

Apollonia Abris Nast's great great grandparents: _Georgii Abriss_ and _Anna Catharina Rapp_.

Apollonia Abriss Nast's great great grandparents: _Joannis Busch_ and _Joannae._

Apollonia Abriss Nast's great great grandparents: _Joannis Nicolai Gerracht_ and _Anna Apolloniae Schardein_

So, we discover that Thomas Nast's mother, Apollonia Abriss was named after her great, great grandmother Anna Apollonia Schardein. It was a very popular name in that region throughout all the years I searched from 1840 back to approximately 1700.

Thomas Nast's father, Joseph Thomas Nast, was a trombonist in the 9th regiment Bavarian Army band at the post where his son Thomas was born, the Red Barracks. Thomas Sr. reportedly arrived in America four years after Thomas and his mother and sister, and he died in 1854. If it is indeed true that Thomas arrived in 1851, then his father died soon after his arrival in the U.S. four years later. If Thomas arrived in 1846, then his father arrived in 1850. I have not found conclusively Mr. Nast Sr.'s death record, but there is no doubt he died in NYC and was buried at Woodlawn Cemetery in the Bronx, although the cemetery cannot confirm this. I base this conclusion on the fact that Thomas and Sarah Nast buried their daughter Julia in this cemetery in 1899 even though they lived in Morristown, New Jersey at the time and had lived there many years when she died. I have, however found a death record for a Thomas Nast, age 50 years and three months, in New York City, Sunday, 13 Mar 1859. This record would fit his profile if he arrived in America in 1855, but there is no way to be sure this was Mr. Nast Sr. While most records from Germany list his name as Joseph Thomas Nast, a couple of his children's birth records listed him simply as Thomas Nast which leads me to think that is the name he went by. I could not find any records for Joseph Thomas Nast's ancestral family other than the parents listed on his marriage record to Apollonia Abriss. The sketch of his father by son Thomas Nast is Illustration 12 at the end of this family section and a sketch of his mother, Apollonia, is Illustration 11. I scanned the tiny drawings from my 1904 edition of Albert Paine's Nast biography and restored them with Paint Shop Pro Photo X2 Ultimate and created the frames with the same program using white borders and filling them with Patterns, then using Effects.

Thomas Nast and Sarah Edwards were married 26 Sep 1861 but I do not have a copy of the marriage document. Pictures of Miss Sarah Edwards in 1859, sketched by her soon to be husband "Tommy", and Thomas Nast in 1859 are Illustrations 1 and 2.

The earliest United States record I have found for Thomas Nast, the artist, is an 1870 Harlem, New York, NY U.S. Federal census at age 29 along with wife Sarah who is also 29, and children Julia age 8, Thomas (Jr) age 5 and Edith age 2. Mr. Nast's occupation is listed as Artist in Oil Painting. His property value is $6,000 and his personal assets are $1,000. Sarah is listed as keeping house. Thomas is listed as being born in Bavaria and is a U.S. citizen. Sarah is listed as being born in PA. All three children are listed as being born in NY. Since he did not purchase the beautiful Morristown, New Jersey home until 1872, he must have owned property in Harlem as well.

On the 1880 Morris County, New Jersey census, the Nast family finds itself in Morristown in the beautiful palatial home called Villa Fontana (See Illustration 14): Thomas is 37, his occupation is listed as artist; Sarah is 38, she keeps house; Julia is 17, attends school; Thomas Jr. is 15, attends school; Edith is 11, attends school; Mabel is 8, she was born in New Jersey, and attends school; Syril [sic] 9/12; Nellie Bogue, age 15, a servant born in Ireland, and Maggie Skelley, age 17, the family cook, also born in Ireland.

For those who are not familiar with genealogy research, the 1890 census was destroyed by fire, an event that causes major distress among researchers to this day. It is also helpful to note that each census year, some different issue is addressed, such as the 1900 census gives the month and year of a person's birth, and how many children a woman has had and how many of them are living.

On the 1900 Morris County, New Jersey census, Thomas Nast was born Sep 1840, is 59, he has been married 49 years (this is obviously a mistake on the part of the census taker) his immigration year was 1851, years in the U.S. is 49, occupation - artist, he can read, write and speak English, he owns his home free and clear. His wife Sarah was born May 1841, she is age 59, she had five children, four of whom are living, she was born in Pennsylvania, both her parents were born in England, she can read, write and speak English. The youngest child, Syril [sic] lives with them. He was born Aug 1879 and is age 20, single, born in New Jersey, his occupation is an insurance agent, he can read, write, and speak English.

Mr. Nast died in 1902. Their daughter Julia died in 1899. Their daughter Edith died in 1909. This was a very harsh decade for the Nast family.

Miss Sarah Edwards was born in Pennsylvania in May 1841. Her parents, George Edwards and Sarah Dearling, were born in England. Sarah was affectionately called Sallie. She and 'Tommy', as Mr. Nast was called by close friends and family, were married 26 Sep 1861when she was 20 years old and Mr. Nast was 21. They enjoyed an ideal marriage by all accounts.

Miss Sarah Edwards is in the household of her parents on the 1850 Philadelphia, PA census at age nine. Her father, George Edwards, is 52 and her mother, Sarah Edwards, is 37. She has a large number of siblings: Helen 25, Louisa 20, both born in England, John 10, Sarah 9, Martha 7, and Eliza 5, all born in Philadelphia. There is a woman from Ireland living with the family as a servant, Jane Forbes age 23. 'Clothing Store' is listed as the occupation and it is listed after the mother Sarah's name. In that time period, it was usual to list the occupation after the head of household's name, usually the father.

On the 1860 New York, NY U.S. Federal census, Miss Sarah Edwards is in the household of David Bruce, along with some of the members of her family. Her father, George Edwards, is 62; her mother, Sarah Edwards, is 48; John is 20, Sarah is 19, Martha is 17, Eliza is 15, and a servant Margaret Swan is 24, also from Ireland as the previous servant was. The Bruce Family also has four servants listed with the members of their family. Helen and Louisa Edwards are no longer with the family. There is no indication about how the Edwards family is related to Mr. Bruce or his wife Matilda. George and Sarah's occupation is listed as 'Furnisher', and once again the designation is listed after Sarah's name, not after her husband's name as is usual for the time period, with ditto marks after George's name, indicating that they worked together in their own business. John Edwards, the brother of Miss Sarah Edwards, is listed as a carpenter.

Miss Sarah Edwards married Thomas Nast 26 Sep 1861 and appears on the 1870 Harlem, New York, NY Federal census with him and three of their children, Julia, Thomas Jr. and Edith. The 1870, 1880, and 1900 censuses are detailed under the information about Thomas Nast.

Sarah Edwards Nast appears on the 1910 Brooklyn, New York, NY Federal census as widow, 68 years old, having five children with three living, so we know a second child has died after Julia died in 1899. Sarah's son Cyril, 30, lives with her as well as her son-in-law Ralph W. St Hill, age 36, a widower, and her grandson Thomas N. 15. So it was Ralph's wife, Edith Nast Porter St Hill that is the second Nast child to die. Edith was the third child of Sarah and Thomas Nast. That must have been extremely hard on the family to lose Julia in 1899, Thomas in 1902, and Edith between 1907 when she married Mr. St Hill and 1910 when the census was taken. Edith Nast Porter married Ralph Woodford St Hill in Manhattan, New York, 27 Apr 1907 so the grandson Thomas N. living with his grandmother Sarah Nast on the 1910 census could not have been Ralph's biological child. A search for Edith's first marriage reveals a marriage for Sarah Edith Nast to Robert H. E. Porter on 26 Sep 1891in Morristown, NJ where the Nast family lived for many years. A birth record for Surname Porter, male, 14 Mar 1894, father Robert H. E. Porter, mother Edith Nast, could very well be the Thomas N. living in the Sarah Nast household in 1910. He would have been listed under Ralph St. Hill since Mr. St. Hill was married to Thomas's deceased mother and possibly this is where the confusion comes in about his last name. Mr. St. Hill may also have adopted Thomas N. after marrying his mother two years before her death. Mr. St. Hill migrated to this country in 1899. See the section on Edith Nast Porter St. Hill.

Widow Sarah E. Nast, age 78, appears on the 1920 Westchester County, New York census in the household of her son Cyril Nast and his family: Cyril 40, Marie S 43, and their son Thomas 5. The initial E. in Sarah's name may stand for Edwards or a middle name. It is interesting to me that the birth record for Edith lists her name as Emily, so Sarah's middle name may have been Emily or Edith. Naming ones female children after the mother was a popular naming pattern of the time. The home is owned and under mortgage. Cyril's occupation is listed as NY Manager – Advertising and he is a wage earner, not an employer.

On the 1930 Westchester, NY census, Sarah is living in the home of her daughter Mabel and Mabel's husband John W Crawford: John 58, Mabel 54, Sarah Nast 88; Kathryn Burns 31 Servant (waiter) from Ireland, Sarah N. Moon 65 Servant (cook) from England; Elizabeth Thompson 52 Practical Nurse from Pennsylvania. John's occupation is Insurance Agent. John and both parents were born in NY.

Mrs. Nast died 20 Oct 1932. Her obituary says she was 92 years of age and had lived at her daughter, Mabel Crawford's home in Beechmont, New Rochelle, New York for the last 19 years. She was also survived by her two sons, Thomas Jr. and Cyril, five grandchildren and eight great grandchildren. Her funeral service was private.

You can find pictures of her grave, as well as Mr. Nast's and some of their children, online at www.findagrave.com in Woodlawn Cemetery, the Bronx New York. I believe this is where Joseph Thomas and Apollonia Abriss Nast are also buried since this is where the Nasts buried their daughter Julia, even though they lived in Morristown, New Jersey, and where they eventually were also buried, Mr. Nast being transferred to Woodlawn in the Bronx from his grave in Ecuador.

To say that Mr. Nast was deeply and romantically in love with his wife throughout all the years of their marriage and that he relied on her as a helpmate in his work would be an understatement. Following is a letter he wrote to her in 1861 from Italy where he engaged in Garibaldie's campaign to free the land. (Courtesy of the Rutherford B. Hayes Presidential Center)

My Dear Sallie:

I have again a letter before my eyes which is written by the one I love so dearly. O, my dear girl, it was a long silence, but I am now again my self.

You write you would like to travel with me, I wish you were with me my darling, but we must wait, and we may travel over the same ground that I am now traveling on. I am very uneasy that you are not well, dear; for heavens sake Sallie, do not get sick. I am afraid you do not go out so often as you used to. You must not stay in the house so much. I wish I were in New York I would take you out everyday; that is to say if somebody would allow me. You read a great many books now, as I see, where there are two, Jersey couple, poor little dear; I miss you. Best thing I can do is to come back to my darling love. You will become homesick. Sallie, I have robbed you of all your pleasure, it is not right. I should not have said a word about loving you, till I got back from my trip, but you will forgive me when I come back, and I hope your pleasure will be restored to you, and live happy as long as you live with me, I do everything I can, which I hope you will believe. Gunn also think I will be successful. Well I am now working hard to be so. You say you wish we have -? Romance of youth sake. My dearest, what am I? I am very poor. The few dollars that I will receive during my stay here, I will spend in Europe, and by the time I come back I am afraid I will be too poor, in fact, too poor to be romantic. Yes, I will have to work very hard again when I return, which will do me no harm, but we will hope the best. So you see my dear, you may be as romantic as you please.

You must not hear what that fool of Gunn says. He is always making you miserable. He is nothing but a nasty beast. You give too much mind to what he says. You must not do it, dear! Your – life as far as I can see will be very happy, at least I will hope so. I for my part will do my best to make you so.

Poor Eliza, it is a shame that she has so much trouble. You will only receive letters when I send to John. You do not go so often to church now, you bad little girl. When I come back I will make you go every Sunday.

Got my sketches done after traveling nearly all day. I am so used up, that I cannot do it even with my best wishes and besides there is always one of the correspondents of the London Times and News with us, and they do it so well that there is no field for me. I have not much time now my dear. I am now working some of my sketches in water colours and we go very often out of town. So you see my time is very much taken up, I have one book which I am now reading by Charles Dickens, "Martin Chuzzlewit". You must not be so afraid about me. I am always in a safe place when the firing commences.

I have had a hard time but it is all over now, that to say as far as I can understand it, there will be no more fighting till next spring, then we go to Venice. What has got into Mattie -? You must not say that you are afraid that you will not be able to write anymore to me. What do you mean, my dear Sallie? If Sol. Eztinge does leave the Office, you may send them in care of Mr. Lexow. Do you know why Sol. Eztinge is going to leave?

To my dearest and best, I will let you know more by my next letter, that is to say what I am going to do, and when I am coming back again. Mr. Thomas writes me that there is a letter for me in London from Mr. Lexow which is of great importance. So when I receive that letter, I will know what I will do this winter. I bid you my dearest good bye till I will write again. I send you my best love and ?.

Your lover,

Thomas (Nast.)

P.S. I send you a picture of myself in the costume which I had on in Calabria. I sent one also to John. Write again soon, my dearest and best.

I think we are safe to assume the man, John, that is mentioned in the letter is Sarah's brother and Eliza is her sister. (See Illustration 3 "Nast As Garibaldian")

Following is a transcription of a letter he wrote to Mrs. Nast and Julia while he was in Washington DC. The date would be between 1863 when Julia was born and July 1865 when Thomas Jr. was born. (Courtesy of the Rutherford B. Hayes Presidential Center)

No. 1 Willard's Hotel

½ past 9. A. M.

Good morning my dearest Sallie and Julia.

I hope you are well.

I kiss you in my imagination. (I wish is reality.) I got to bed after 12:00 last night. Had tea about a half an hour before. Kissed your forehead before I lay down and said goodnight to it. Could not get to sleep for some time thinking of you, your cold feet, and wishing that I could warm them. - Got up this morning at 7, my room is number 253 up I do not know how many stairs. Had breakfast at 8 – My want you here very much, my do not know how to sharpen knifes, do not know how to keep the meals warm. O darling, it is hard for a man to travel, that has so comfortable home as – well as – as – I have got. I was sorry that I washed myself before I went to the table, because is napkin was damp enough to wash myself with, all I was in need of was <u>soap</u>. Do not see a soul in the hotel that I know. Good bye for the present. Will write again soon. Kisses for you both. God bless you. I – I – I wish I was home. I may never - never will leave my wooden shanty in 125th W 2nd House W 5th Ave Good bye. O, I may write a few more lines about how g——-tly? the servants wake up their guests for the different trains. At 4 this morning I was rise from my sleep by a bang – bang – bang. I thought is some —————-? But when I got to my senses I found it was a servant waking my next door neighbor, "Four o'clock, Sir". A faint voice in the room "O – O- O yes, alright." Then the sweet servant went away not on a light fantastic toe but as if had shoes made of wood, and very many legs in them, the step got fainter and fainter which lasted some five minutes) but this was not the only time he came, every half hour in the same general way till I go up to the White House 20 min to 11. I arrive at the White House. G Hayes and Nicholo was glad to see me – liked my pictures very much. The President came in the room, was introduced, shook hands, seemed in a hurry to go. Gave him the letter (Curtiss's) Did not open it and left but seemed pleased to see me, that is to say what he did see on me. Nicolo is a German by birth born not four miles from Landow (where I was born). Hayes had to go out, I am waiting for his return. Said something about painting a picture for the capitol and Hayes will find out how I can get it. So far good but I am afraid it will be no go. Will try to see the President again. Better luck next time. Would like to have a few words with him, he is very busy, quite a number of men in this room to see him, some are very ——- ones I can assure you. One tall man came in, made a great deal of noise, without any necktie and hat, rather a loose appearance, got tired of waiting and walked off. The c——-? and things in general are very shabby, do not have a look of greatness which a house like this should have. Good bye my darling for a time. God bless you. I wish you was here. I think things would go better -

Following is the transcription of a letter from Mr. Nast to Mrs. Nast in 1863. It makes a reference about his mother and is the only record I have found in the United States for her. From this letter, it is clear she was still alive in July 1863. It is also probable that she either lived with him and Sarah, or close by since he asked Sarah to say hello for him. (Courtesy of the Rutherford B. Hayes Presidential Center)

Harrisburg July 3rd 9 P.M. 1863

My dearest darling wife,

I am under arrest – Now I will tell you all about this morning. I went to the ———- to get a pass. The Governor gave me a letter to Gen. Couch, and he was to give me the pass. So I was waiting outside for an answer, who should come as prisoner but our beloved cousin Henry (a armed man on each side of him). We exchanged words and asked him if he joined the rebels, he being dressed different from our soldiers. He is a captain. He told me no, but this was the third time that he was arrested and he got up a company in Philadelphia.

The officers seeing me told to him instead of giving me a pass, passed me to the Provost Marshal, with a orderly. I was taking to the coms house where he was and he asked me if I know the prisoner. He the prisoner was not there at the time. I told the Marshal all I knew of him. He had no doubt that I was innocent but he would put a man under me till 3 the afternoon, and he would examine me.

The jury man that had me in charge was not armed and I was allowed to go to my dinner at the hotel. Three o'clock came and I saw Henry again. At first he did not see but when he did he asked me ——— what I did here. I told him. He said "Is not this jolly." I could not see it, staying nearly all day in that Hot doing nothing.

It seems that he has stolen horses, killed a calf, and had a rebel signal flag on his person. He behaved very badly during the trial, laughing speaking loud, and would talk to me. I told him that I did not want say anything more to me, and he should behave. He behaved better after a while. The ex———-? of some German farmers and it was very funny that part of it. About sunset they adjourned and we were to be there at 8 this evening.

I found out by the man that had me in charge that General Stahel was in town so I called on him to say a word for me which he did do.

Gen. Stahel is very much disgusted about things in general, he said that just on the eve of battle where he could have ———-? a victory, he was relieved of his command and sent to take charge of the cavalry in that department. He is here to take charge but he cannot find any cavalry to take charge of. He said that when he took leave of his men that a great number of them cried. He loved his men and they loved him, but he is a ———- forever and he must not get higher in rank, which he would have done had he won a victory. He as yet had not lost any fight and that is sad.

Well, Gen. Stahel called on the Marshal at 8 this evening and it made an impression on the Marshal, that I was alright but still he could not release me. My man said I had better go to tea without him. He knew I would be there in time. Well the trial lasted another hour and the Marshal said I had better go to my hotel without my jury man here in the morning at 8. How long this trial will last I cannot say so I went night afraid to the hotel and commenced writing to my dear loving wife and relieve my mind.

Henry said he has not had anything to eat for two days, his feet are very sore and he has several fresh wounds on his body.

I hope they will discharge me in the morning so I could go and dine with John. By the way he is alright up to tonight. I have seen men from the front in his regiment today, and they say none of the men have been wounded or killed although they have had a little fighting.

It is raining very hard, thundering and lightning and I wish I was I was once more in 89 Street 5 ½ house from 1st Ave.

How is my dear little love? I hope well. Is Julia alright? Tomorrow is the 4th and I do so wish you will enjoy yourself. Now do not get ——heart about me. I will be alright very soon, I think tomorrow or so. It has been very warm here and I have been suffering all day. If things do not improve soon I will be in town before the 7th and go with you (to) Rochester that would be nice. You would like that and so would I. Now if you was with me to comfort me, kiss me a little, I would be alright, but here I will have to go to bed without comfort. O, my, you have disabled me from this kind of life and made a homebody of me. Give my love to your mother (mine also) Martha and Eliza. My kisses for you and Julia on the paper. Good night dear love. May God bless you and Julia and ——? Your loving husband

Tommy

The area of Europe that Mr. Nast was born was the land of his parent's fathers and their fathers before them. The German name 'Nast' was a topographical name for someone who lived in a thickly wooded area, or an occupational name for a woodcutter. It is from Middle High German meaning a branch as from a tree. The area where Mr. Nast was born was on the edge of the largest forest in Europe. Landau was first mentioned in history as a settlement in 1106 AD and the general area was exchanged back and forth between France and Germany over the centuries. The area was under French rule from 1680-1815 during the period that Mr. Nast's great, great, great grandparents Joannis Busch and his wife Joannae, and Joannis Nicolai Gerracht and his wife Anna Apolloniae Schardein lived around 1700 AD. Landau was granted to Bavaria in 1816. Mr. Nast mother Apollonia Abriss was born in 1801 and married Mr. Joseph Thomas Nast in 1834. There is no doubt Mr. Nast's family was well aware of the turmoil of the area.

They were a part of the land, and that land had been soaked in blood and violence for centuries. Although there are no accurate numbers for the millions of people Charlemagne killed if they refused to become Catholic, the number generalized is 50 million over a span of 30 years. It is said he beheaded 4,500 Saxons in one day and his reign is described as rivers of blood. Napoleon is said to be responsible for four million deaths. There is no doubt with this kind of terror in their past, the ancestors of Mr. Nast handed down family stories that influenced the man that Thomas Nast became.

No doubt the threat and fear caused by the instability of the region caused Mr. Joseph Thomas Nast concern when he saw the danger building around them in 1846 and decided to send his family to safety before the 1848 European Revolution spread throughout Europe from its starting point in France. The long history of the Nast family on the French/German border would have put them right in the eye of the storm, had they stayed, in which tens of thousands of people were killed.

No realistic appraisal of Thomas Nast would be complete without addressing the claims by some that he plagiarized photographers in the battlefields of the Civil War, he himself working in his studio. It cannot be said that Mr. Nast avoided the battlefields of the Civil War because of cowardice, for he joined Garibaldi's struggle to free Sicily and Italy while in Europe, sketching his way through the battles with little or no money, returning home in 1860 with fifty cents in his pocket, and returning to Europe with his family 19 years later, a man of means. (See Nast as Garibaldi Illustration 3)

It is simply a fact that his original job was to polish rough sketches from the field; this was his paid position and was not plagiarism. But his powerful, emblematic pictures that stirred the hearts of citizen and soldier alike were his own. James Pamos, a close friend and associate, said that he personally sat by Mr. Nast many times while he was drawing and also during those electric moments when an idea for a picture was conceived, and he attests to the fact that the pictures were an integral part of both Mr. Nast's mind and his hand. It was not until the war was over that his pictures became caricatures. The fertility of invention displayed by the artist, week after week, for months at a time, was so extraordinary that people concluded the ideas must be furnished to him by others. All one has to do is look at the elaborate detail in "The Same Old Christmas Story Over Again" to realize you are looking into a limitless mind of great creativity. The picture holds innumerable scenes such as Gulliver's Travels replete with all the little people, Little Bo Peep and her sheep, Little Red Riding Hood and the wolf, The Cat and the Fiddle with the cow jumping over the moon, pirates, ship wrecks, Santa and his reindeer, plus many, many more all playing around in the dreams of two children asleep on Christmas Eve. There are fantasy figures playing in and out of the girl and boy's hair, and a little bird pecking at her nose. It is almost beyond belief that anyone could accomplish all that tiny, intricate work with a pencil and paper. This one drawing alone is enough to heap accolades on Mr. Nast's imagination and talent in transferring that amazing image from mind to paper. Likewise a drawing of Mother Goose playing a piano surrounded by a roomful of children just dazzles the intellect with endless excursions into the fantasy palace of the brain. I did not include these pictures in this book because I could not envision myself spending the hours, days, and weeks it would take me to re sketch them, but you can find them online.

If one is honest while comparing Mr. Nast's artwork to the work of Civil War photographers such as Matthew Brady or field sketch artists, it is like comparing apples to oranges, both wonderful but having nothing in common other than the Civil War. When one looks at the extensive and delicate detail in such works displayed under the Art of Thomas Nast section of this book, the breadth and depth of Mr. Nast imagination and ability to manifest that imagination through pen or pencil to wood block, blackboard, or paper is only eclipsed by the great master himself, Michael Angelo.

Mr. Nast studied as a young teenager with the German-born history painter Theodore Kaufmann and at the National Academy of Design for a short time. He began to work for Leslie's Illustrated Weekly Magazine when he was just a boy of 15 in 1855. He then worked for Harper's Weekly in 1859 and 1860, returning to work for them when he returned from Europe after an assignment to England by Leslie's and then over to Italy to join Garibaldie's army. His return to Harper's brought him to fame and into the company of great men such as President Grant and his friend Mark Twain, both of whom were guests at his home. It was actually bad investments at the behest of President Grant that lost both Grant and Mr. Nast their wealth. Mr. Nast invested his entire fortune in a book publishing company of Grant and Ward, and when it failed in 1884, he was left nearly penniless.

When his fortunes fell to desperate levels, he was offered a job at a certain newspaper if he would confine himself to their editorial policy and he refused, saying he "could not outrage his convictions." Mr. Nast continued to keep his cheerful nature and strong wit throughout his life, as well as his adherence to patriotism and respect for law and order.

Some interesting incidentals about Mr. Nast's personal life that I uncovered during the last five years are as follows: Mr. Nast was a talented organist. A mountain peak was named for him in Colorado, 12,454 feet Mt. Nast. He owned a mine in the Black Hills, and he played poker. When a Chicago reporter asked him as to whether Mr. Nast enjoyed Chicago, a picture of a boned turkey, champagne gin cocktails, and fried calumet snipe quickly followed, perhaps a view into his culinary tastes. Mr. Nast had a skeleton that he used in many of his sketches. He kept it in a glass case along with his musket and other war relics. His family was familiar with arriving home from an outing and finding the skeleton sitting in a chair as a model for one or another of his pictures. Of the many images in which he used the skeleton, I chose one to include in this book, Illustration 10, "There is nothing mean about us", denoting a skin and bones military through Congressional cuts. Mr. Nast was wholly dedicated to the idea that peace comes through a strong defense. I chose this particular military picture because of the parallels it holds to our military stretched thin today, but my favorite 'skeleton drawing' is the one about California, "Social Science Solved" in which the skeleton, wearing a ribbon across his chest that says Communism, is demonstrating on the street holding a flag that says ANARCHY and a banner proclaiming California's new Constitution supporting Common Stock in the Universal Co-Operative Brotherhood. The political button on his hat says Free Love and his hatband says 'Deadheadism', a term that Mr. Nast used to designate a doctrine held by people who want a free ride.

Mr. Nast had letterhead stationary which he used as note paper, the date on the letterhead being1887/1888 and transcribed as follows:

<table>
<tr><td>1887</td><td></td><td>1888</td></tr>
</table>

First
TOUR OF THE PACIFIC STATES
Under the management of
Lewis R. Villemaire

Th: Nast

(Under the signature is a self sketched image of Mr. Nast. On each side of the image is information):

(On the left it says):	(On the right it says):
Th. Nast,	This attraction is now booked
Artistic Entertainment	with First Class Houses only.
Drawing in	All communications
Black and White	Addressed to
AND PAINTING IN	Louis R. VILLEMAIRE
OIL COLORS	Manager
IN THE PRESENCE OF THE AUDIENCE	

(Courtesy of the Rutherford B. Hayes Presidential Center)

But of all the bits of trivia I have discovered about Mr. Nast, the one I enjoyed most was that he had a mocking bird in a cage in his study. His grandson, Thomas Nast St. Hill, related that the bird would toss gravel at his grandfather when he became engrossed in his work and ignored the bird. When Mr. Nast would go upstairs to his study, the bird would whistle at him and he would whistle back. There is a picture of Mr. Nast's studio at the end of this family section taken after his death showing the bird cage nearby his desk. (See Illustration 10) I wondered how the bird could have tossed gravel from this distance and vantage point, but subsequently I was privileged to view a photo of Mr. Nast sitting at his desk, and the birdcage is sitting above him on top of the back of the desk. In a letter from Mr. Nast to his wife while he was struggling alone in Ecuador shortly before his death from Yellow Fever in December, 1902, he mentions that he "misses the bird too" in reply to her pen that his mockingbird misses him.

September 21, 1902. – "You say my poor old mocking bird misses me. I'm very sorry. I do miss him, poor fellow, and his mocking sounds."

One article in particular I found valuable for its peek into the personal family life of Mr. Nast, as well as a description of how he produced his drawings, by Eli Perkins during a visit to the Nast home in Morristown. He describes his commute by train from the Christopher Street ferry over the New Jersey salt meadows, and through the Morris and Essex Tunnel as taking sixty minutes. Mr. Nast met him at the depot and they walked the half mile to Villa Fontana. He describes the home as being filled with pictures, home comforts, and four little angel babies, and presiding over all this happiness was a young Yankee wife with brown hair, graceful form, and delicate damask cheeks. He notes that Julia is the oldest child, Thomas Jr. is eight, then Edith, and that Mabel is a toddler. He compares Mrs. Nast to Mrs. Buchanan Read, the wife of the dead poet-painter. Out of curiosity, I did an image search for Mrs. Read and indeed she does have the alabaster porcelain look of Mrs. Nast. Buchanan Read painted The Harp of Erin in 1867, a beautiful painting of a woman sitting on a rock in the sea playing a golden harp. You might notice that the artists of the time all idealized women with long flowing hair and angelic features, like Columbia, the symbol of America so prevalent in Mr. Nast pictures. Mr. Perkins continues with his story about visiting the family at Villa Fontana, being left with Mrs. Nast and four year old Mabel (Mabel was eight years old when Cyril, the youngest child, was born in 1879) while Mr. Nast went to his studio momentarily; Mabel prattled away as she looked at Mr. Perkins through her German haircut, erstwhile playing the piano keys with her little hands and telling him that "Papa had bought new furniture for the parlor." After lunch, they went to the studio where Mr. Nast worked. The room was filled with sketches and drawings by some of art's great masters. (See Illustration 10 - Nast Studio). There was a table in the studio on which the images were drawn on a block of wood. They were sent to town where they were divided into several pieces, so that several workmen could engrave on them at once. It would have taken one workman two weeks to engrave a picture the size of Harper's Weekly at a cost of about $100. Since Mr. Nast had to produce a picture every week, time was of the essence. Mr. Perkins asked if Mr. Nast had made a good deal of money to which he replied that he had never made a cent outside his small professional pay. His dry humor shows through when he explains he cannot afford to live in town, that Morristown is a fashionable summer resort whose fashionable residents spend winters in the city. He then quips that last summer they were very fashionable but this winter they are not so fashionable, and asks, "Are we, dear?" of his wife. Mrs. Nast replies, "No, Tom, but the children are healthy and we are very happy."

When Mr. Perkins asked if others gave him his ideas, Mr. Nast said that no they did not, although he did get a lot of mail with suggestions. He said, laughing, that he had received a genuine proposition of marriage from an admiring young lady in Ohio, so he drew a cartoon of Mrs. Nast and the children, labeled 'the only objections' which he sent back to her.

That Mr. & Mrs. Nast had a close, loving, and enduring marriage is evident in the many articles I read, as well as in Mr. Paine's biography of Mr. Nast. On an anniversary trip to the site of their honeymoon, Niagara Falls, after many years of marriage, it was reported by observers that they were so lighthearted and happy they appeared to be on a second honeymoon. A letter that 'Sallie' and 'Tommy' wrote to her parents while on their honeymoon in 1861 is splattered with his drawings of events and functions they engaged in while at Niagara Falls.

On one occasion after her husband's death in 1902, Mrs. Nast was sued over one of her husband's paintings. The complaint stated that Henry P. Toler purchased the painting of The Christ Head in 1900 for $1500 and subsequently sold it to the complainants. Mrs. Nast countered that her husband had used the painting as collateral for a loan, the painting presently being in her possession, but the complainants said this was merely because Mr. Toler had returned the painting to Mr. Nast for touchups.

The many pictures taken by others of Mr. Nast at different times in his life show the different stages of his lifelong cause against wrong etched on his face and in the expression of his eyes. Like those of us familiar with taking a stand against injustice, one starts out ready to take on the world. As time passes, and although some battles are won, the injustice of this world gradually wears us down. In the 1859 picture, Mr. Nast looks self assured, almost cocky in his determination to wage war on corruption. (Illustration 1) In 1877 he has a look of cautious determination, not quite ready to throw in the towel, but reflective nonetheless about the many fronts of injustice that continue to crop up regardless of his efforts. (Illustration 5) This picture reminds me of the old television program "The Untouchables" about Eliot Ness and the war on Chicago's prohibition crime syndicate in the 1920s. He also was incorruptible as Mr. Nast was incorruptible and broke the backs of the crime syndicate just as Mr. Nast broke the crime syndicate in New York His older pictures show a look in the eyes of sadness, not necessarily of defeat, but that he did his best and there was still much left to do, and he was not able to do it. Mr. Nast's self portraits showed a scrappy and rascally little man, some defiant and others angry, that defied his enemies, which were also the enemies of what is good and right. (Illustration 7)

Villa Fontana, the Nast home in New Jersey, had extensive grounds with pathways meandering throughout, a fountain, bushes and flowers, a sweeping veranda, all draped in vines at every turn, filled with family love and harmony. Inside the stately home it was replete with art objects; some Mr. Nast bought and others were gifts. The years he spent there were filled with love of home and family, as well as being the center of his work place. A family photo album shows the family engaged in a lot of activities such as bicycling, croquet, hunting, baseball, tennis, traveling and sightseeing, You could say his home and family was where his heart dwelled in every aspect of his life and few knew the sacrifice it was for him to accept the job in Ecuador in 1902 that would lead to his death. It was only financial necessity that drove him to leave his happy life. It was a tremendous hardship to be away from his wife upon whom he relied in so many ways, but he feared she might contract the Yellow Fever that was prevalent in Ecuador so he went alone.

Mr. Nast was working on the painting of "Lee Awaiting Grant" when he was called to accept the Consul appointment in Ecuador. It was hoped to be the masterpiece of his extensive historical paintings. (See Illustration 17)The painting was unfinished, and un named, when he left and was later titled by his family. In the foreground of the big canvas sits the vanquished Confederate leader, his gray head bowed in despair, and his eyes fixed upon the half unsheathed sword across his knees – the swore presented to him by the State of Virginia, and the sword he must soon surrender to the leader of the northern army. In the background are two figures – at the right, Colonel Marshall, Lee's aide, and at the left Captain Babcock, one of Grant's aides, who arranged the meeting. The scene of the picture is a room in McLean's farmhouse at Appomattox. Mr. Nast went there and made sketches of the place to help him in the painting.

Covering the greater part of one wall of the parlor at Villa Fontana is an imposing mantle over the fireplace called the Shakespearian mantle by the family. Mr. Nast patiently gathered the tiles over a number of years and grouped them in pictures and scenes from Shakespeare so harmonious that it presents a memorial to Shakespeare. Just above the fireplace and beneath the mantelshelf is a carved box cover that came from Shakespeare's house. Mr. Nast had to buy the whole box to get the cover. Across a strip of highly polished brass running the width of the open fireplace is Shakespeare's epithet:

> *Good friend for Jesus sake forbeare*
> *To dig the dust encloased heare*
> *Blest be ye man yt spares thes stones*
> *And cursed be he yt moves my bones.*

There is another unique mantelpiece and fireplace in the dining room called the Sixpence after the Mother Goose rhyme "Sing a Song of Sixpence". The tiles that make up this mantle, display pictures of the king, queen, maid, and blackbirds and were made in England over two hundred years previous to 1903.

Of the many treasures that filled his home, one of the most valued was the silver vase presented to him by our military forces bearing the following inscription:

"Presented to Thomas Nast by his friends of the Army and Navy of the United States, in recognition of the patriotic use which he has made of his rare abilities as an artist of the people. The gift of three thousand five hundred officers and enlisted men of the Army and Navy of the United States."

In 1908, Mrs. Nast donated another silver vase to the Metropolitan Museum of Art that was presented to Mr. Nast in 1869 by members of the New York Union League Club, along with a gold locket. The inscription on the vase read: "To Thomas Nast – A token of admiration of his genius, and of his ardent devotion of that genius to the preservation of his country from the schemes of rebellion." The locket was presented to Mr. Nast in Denver in 1887. On one side is an etched portrait of the artist and on the other side a base-relief of the Mountain of the Holy Cross, as it looks from Denver. It was modeled in the several different metals that are mined in Colorado. Mr. Nast had an ongoing close relationship with the state of Colorado, as numerous newspaper articles did attest.

In 1915, Mrs. Nast donated two of Mr. Nast's Civil War paintings to the War Department. The larger painting entitled Saving the Flag bears the legend, "Song of the volunteers: We are coming Father Abraham, 300 thousand more." The other painting is entitled, "Peace Again" and is based on Gen. U.S. Grant's magnanimous order at the surrender of Lee's army at Appomattox: "Let them take their horses with them; they will need them for the spring plowing."

Probably the greatest sadness for Mr. Nast in his lifetime was the death of his first child, daughter Julia, and the unnecessary and erroneous comments that swirled around her death. I wonder what he would say was his greatest moment. Most people would say the exposure and ultimate destruction of the Tammany Ring of corruption in New York would be his number one achievement, but I think he would say his role as a husband and father and patriot was his crowning glory.

The Children

Julia Nast

Julia Nast was born in 1863 in New York City and lived into her adulthood at her family's home in Morristown, New Jersey after they moved there in 1872 when she was about nine years of age. She is on the 1870 Harlem, New York census, age 8, and the Morristown, New Jersey1880 census, age 17, in the household of her father Mr. Nast. Since we do not have the 1890 census available to us because it was destroyed by fire, I have found only four records for Julia prior to her death in 1899. The 1870 census record lists 1862 as her birth year while the 1880 census lists her birth year as 1863, but the newspaper articles about her death say she was 35 at the time of her death in 1899. Without a birth record, which I have been unable to find, old records can be misleading. She was buried in Woodlawn Cemetery in the Bronx, section 37, Lot # 1249, Spruce Plot.

As a young child, she wrote a two page letter to her father on small notepaper while he was away on a lecture tour, probably at the same time as the letter her brother Thomas Jr. wrote that you will find transcribed in his section following Julia's. That letter was written in 1872 since Mabel was born in December 1871 and Thomas Jr. talks about her learning to talk in his letter to Papa. Julia decorated the top of the first page with the head of a wolf. She drew one stamp on the small envelope with the words Dear Papa along with two ladies facing each other extending hands in greeting. One of the women has a headdress on. On the back of the envelope she drew the head of a wolf that matched the one on the letterhead. On the last page after her signature she drew a picture of a woman and wrote that it was Ruth with her different hair on. The letter reads:

Dear Papa,

I wish your eyes wher [sic] better but it is no use wishing. That will not help it. What time do you think you will be home when you come? You know that picture you sent Mama? Don't you. I put it in my scrap book. I have got lots of little pictures in it. They look real nice. I think I have no no [sic] more to say so I will stop. From Julia (Courtesy of the Rutherford B. Hayes Presidential Center)

In the articles about Julia's death, her friends say she had a good head on her shoulders and was solid as a rock. I think her letter to Papa gives us some insight into her personality and shows her to be a pragmatic realist.

In a second small snippet of information in another newspaper article about her and a group of other young girls participating in a Young Maiden's Cooking Association in 1881 at the Nast home, Julia is the head cook and is said to be quite talented at it. She would have been 18 years old.

By a wonderful stroke of luck, one of the pieces of correspondence I requested from the Hayes Presidential Center elaborated on Julia's cooking skills. The piece is most probably by Jeannette Gilder who contributed a regular column, The Lounger, to the Critic, a bi-weekly journal of review that she and her brother Joseph started in 1881:

The Critic

February 12, 1887
The Lounger

I have heard of a luncheon given by a well known caricaturist recently to a company of fellow artists that possessed several unique features.

The host, who lives in an old and attractive New Jersey town, entertained his guests with a most elaborately cooked repast, which was served by two unusually attractive waitresses in coquettish caps. As artists are an unconventional class, the guests did not hesitate to compliment the host upon each course as it appeared – and disappeared. At the end of the meal the host said that as they had expressed so much pleasure in the luncheon, they might be interested in the cook, and that if they didn't mind he would introduce her.

After the coffee and cigars they adjoined to the drawing room, where the cook entered leaning upon the host's arm; for it was his eldest daughter who had prepared the whole meal with her own fair hands.

One of the artists asked that the waitresses whom he shrewdly suspected to be the younger daughters be brought in, but his request was not heeded. No luncheon ever served at Delmonico's was more highly praised than this one, or more thoroughly enjoyed. (Courtesy of the Rutherford B. Hayes Presidential Center)

Julia died 28 Apr 1899 at age 35 in the city of her birth. I found some old newspaper articles from 1899 about her death on the Library of Congress Web site. There were rumors that she died from a cocaine overdose. There were rumors she committed suicide. The coroner found that she died from natural causes; did not kill herself and did not die from a drug overdose. By all accounts she had a good strong mind and was well grounded. She was a nurse in New York City and had been employed for a year under contract. When the year was finished, she went home to Morristown and spent some time with her parents. She then gained a new contract for work and moved back to New York in the same boarding house she had lived in during the previous employment. It had to be excruciatingly painful for Mr. and Mrs. Nast to endure the agony of their first child's death under the shadow of all the innuendos. Mr. Nast had made some viral enemies over the years for his courageous stand against corruption, including those in the newspaper business, especially in New York City, and it must have weighed heavily on his mind that some of the negative comments about Julia's death were hateful actions against him. The headlines screamed the day after her death that the daughter of the 'formerly' well-known cartoonist was killed by cocaine before anyone knew the true cause, jumping to this conclusion because no reason was known as to why she would kill herself, another illogical and premature assumption. If indeed Julia used cocaine, that substance was in many home remedy medicines and was in common use at that time. It was advertised in toothache drops in 1885, and in 1886, it was the main ingredient in the newly formed soft drink Coca Cola. It wasn't until 1920 that cocaine was outlawed by the Dangerous Drug Act.

According to all the articles I found about Julia's death, she was staying at her former landlady's boarding house in New York City, Mrs. Elizabeth Ginnis at 31 East Twenty-second Street, the same place she had stayed the previous year during her former engagement of work as a professional nurse. Julia had graduated five years prior to her death from the Bellevue Hospital Training School. Julia had gone to spend some time with her parents at the end of that last job. She had returned to New York and found a new job. She had gotten a very bad head cold, and also suffered from insomnia. She had told her friends that she was under medical treatment. Late on Saturday night, having heard her walking about her room, Mrs. Ginnis's sister went to inquire after her and she replied she was fine, just could not sleep. Not coming down to breakfast Sunday morning, the maid went to see about her and she was in the last moments of life. A letter on the side table was addressed to Julia's brother-in-law, Robert Porter, her sister Edith's husband, whom Mrs. Ginnis immediately sent for. The letter, according to Mr. Porter, was a reminder that he had promised to lend Julia some money and asked him to send it at his earliest convenience. There was no mention of suicide in the letter. Mr. Porter and her brother Thomas Nast Jr. had Julia's body removed to an undertaking establishment on West Twenty-third Street and an autopsy was to be held by Deputy Coroner O'Hanlon. The autopsy revealed Julia had died of natural causes. Another article surmised she had a romance in her life from another touching letter found by her bedside addressed to a woman friend that disclosed she was in love with a married man and he with her. Julia was very beautiful and wore attractive clothing and stylish hats. I could have chosen a better picture of Julia for this book but I chose the picture of her carrying rakes, while her sister Edith mowed the lawn in the same picture. It gives a good insight into just how large the grounds of Villa Fontana were and that the girls helped care for the property, as well as giving the reader an idea of what they looked like. I dated the picture about 1888 since the girls look to be in their early twenties and Edith was married in 1891 at age 23. See Illustration 16 (Courtesy of the Rutherford B. Hayes Presidential Center). Sadly, both these beautiful young women would die an early death; both Julia and Edith died at age 35.

The picture of Mrs. Nast and her first baby Julia in 1863, Illustration 4, was originally sketched by Mr. Nast. I scanned the small sketch from my Nast biography by Mr. Paine and enlarged, restored, and painted it with PSP X2. I did put the reflection in the mirror but otherwise it is an accurate duplication. I created the frame by using white borders and filling them with a pattern of the picture itself and creating effects.

Mr. Nast used his children as models for many of his drawings. His pictures manifested amazingly accurate portrayals of facial expressions, even their eyes which are the most difficult feature to capture and duplicate time and again. It is easy to identify the drawings in which he used his children by their ages, especially the first three, Julia, Thomas Jr., and Edith, when they appear in a picture together. They frequent his Santa Claus images, and many show the inside of their Villa Fontana home in Morristown; the staircase, the moldings, the wainscoting, the hardwood floors and rugs give an insight into their life in that beautiful old house. One of the pictures Mr. Nast drew of the children waiting for Santa includes a little dog; they actually did have a little dog that looks quite like the drawing. I debated whether to include a restored painting of it but again, I wanted to keep the number of illustrations to an affordable number for most people. I believe the people in the picture are Thomas Jr. by the chair with Mabel asleep in the chair, and Mr. and Mrs. Nast peeking in the door at them. The little dog is by the chair. The children in the older group were born in 1863, Julia, 1865, Thomas Jr., and 1868, Edith, so identifying them in pictures when they are together is quite easy, as well as the second group of children, Mabel, Dec. 1871and Cyril, Aug 1879 when they appear together.

Thomas Nast Jr.

Thomas Nast Jr. was born in 1865. In a handwritten letter to his father as a very young child, Thomas Jr. illustrated the letter in the same style as his father. The letter was on four small note pages. The envelope on the front said Papa Nast and had four hand drawn stamps on it. On the back, Thomas Jr. said, "I was afraid my letter wouldn't go so I put so many stamps on it." The letter was written in the hand of a young child with lead pencil and some misspelled words, a couple of which are indecipherable. On the first page of the letter to the left of the date was drawn a beautifully perfect rose, stem, leaves, and a bud that is excellent in form and shading. At the end of the letter we are fortunate to learn the pet name Mr. Nast called his son, Tomothy Topkins. The letter begins:

March 14, Dear Papa, Do you hate leturing [sic] yet? Mother is getting lonely some. You will miss Mabel's __ingist. She is just leaning how to talk She can say Tom quite plain and she can say Ediht [sic] and Julia and Gin and Bill. She says them real funny. Aren't you coming home in April? Mama is going to New York with Mrs. Parker if it is a fine day. Do you take your sleep? I wrote a letter I told her to Mrs Babbott and told her to come and stay a week. She was hear [sic] and stade [sic]? and Mama wanted her to stay and told her not to be baley [sic]. Good by from your Tomothy Topkins. Th Nast Jr. (Courtesy of the Rutherford B. Hayes Presidential Center)

In the fall of 1886, Mr. Nast visited his son, Thomas Jr. in Colorado for two months. The son was a mining engineer in that state.

Thomas Jr. is not living in the household of his father Thomas Nast Sr. on the 1895 New Jersey State Census. The only one of the children remaining in the household is Cyril.

Thomas Nast Jr. married Ella Bogart Shields on 1 Jan 1897 New York, NY.

His marriage record does not correspond to the 1900 Manhattan, New York census on which the census taker reports Thomas Jr. and Ella have been married seven years with a marriage year of 1893. The only way I can explain this error is possibly the census taker had auditory dyslexia and reversed the numbers. On that 1900 census Thomas Jr., 35, is living with his wife Ella, 34, in Manhattan. They have no children. He was born in July 1865 and she was born in Dec 1866. A servant lives with them, Mary Thompson, age 24, Black, born in New York in Sep 1876.

A four page playbill in 1901-1902 for a year long artistic entertainment tour which I found on the Library of Congress Web site, is transcribed as follows through the courtesy of Records of the Redpath Chautauqua Bureau, University of Iowa Libraries, Iowa City, Iowa:

Page I – *Thos: Nast Jr. Ambidextrous Caricaturist ... 137 Times in New York City 1901—1902 UNDER SOLE MANAGEMENT Southern Lyceum Bureau Louisville, Atlanta, Dallas*

I created the picture of Thomas Nast Jr. in Illustration 15 at the end of the Family Section of this book from Page I of this playbill.

Page II - *Daily Reminders of Th: Nast. And Ambidextrous Drawing BY HIS SON Thos: Nast Jr.*

This entertainment will illustrate and reproduce the many ideas of the late Thomas Nast that have become indispensable to the art of pictorial expression, giving the history and recalling the circumstances under which so many of the things we see every day were originated in the exhaustless mind of this wonderful man. This artist and diplomat; this destroyer of corruption; this greatest political cartoonist the world has ever known; one of this county's most ardent patriots, who may justly be ranked with Washington, Lincoln, and Grant.

Thos: Nast, Jr., will also give an exhibition of his ambidextrous drawing which has entertained, amused, and astonished his audiences. A rival of no one, he has entered a field unoccupied, wherein he demonstrates that he has not only inherited a rich measure of his lamented father's great talent, but is also able to accomplish a wonderful feat in ambidexterity, thus enabling him to give the unique and instructive entertainments he is now presenting.

Page III – (Reviews) *New York: Herald – Mr. Thomas Nast Jr. gave an interesting exhibition of ambidextrous drawing; Tribune – Thomas Nast Jr. … This week's feature; Telegraph – He shows steady improvement … of real value … a crown of laurels awaiting him so large he would have to take it home in a cab; Hotel Gazette – He is a worthy successor to his father; Daily American – He is a handsome fellow, a clever artist and score easily. Chicago, IL: Tribune – Thomas Nast Jr., son of the famed cartoonist is one of the chief attractions. He does some remarkable drawing … for the fact that he uses both hands, drawing with either equally well, and frequently employing both at the same time, and making two different sketches; Record Herald - … gives evidence of singular dexterity, much artistic ability, and wonderful determination; Chronicle – Thomas Nast Jr. has a most unique specialty; Daily News – The ambidextrous caricatures of Thomas Nast forms one of the most unique specialties seen … this season. Philadelphia, PA: The Record - … making a decided hit … the prime novelty – Mr. Nast Jr. shows that he has inherited no small degree of his father's deftness; Inquirer - … is highly entertaining; Item - … attracts thousands of artists; The Times – successful where he has appeared in public. Boston, Mass: Herald – One of the most wonderful acts was the ambidextrous caricature works of Thomas Nast Jr. … he is a genuine novelty; Daily Globe – Medical men would declare such a feat almost impossible, and the physical condition that enables this artist to make use of both his hands and eyes at the same time and in different directions makes his drawing nothing short of wonderful; Journal – He is ambidextrous and very cleaver; Daily Advertiser – Thomas Nast Jr., son of the great cartoonist is one of the special attractions; Courier - Tom Nast Jr., son of the world famous caricaturist, inheriting in rich measure his father's talent; Times – a laughable and clever specialty; Post – Tom Nast Jr. who will be as well known as his illustrious father as a cartoonist and caricaturist. Providence, RI: Evening Bulletin – Thomas Nast Jr., one of the celebrated caricaturists, does a particularly skillful act of crayon sketching. He uses both hands at once; The News - … the finest act of the kind … highly appreciated … He has a pleasing stage presence and an ease of manner that is delightful. Detroit, Mich: Free Press – One of the truly attractive and artistic incidents is the appearance of Thos. Nast Jr. as a picture maker. This artist has hit upon a novel and fetching act, and it possesses the uncommon qualities of refinement and entertainment. The drawing of two pictures simultaneously – one with either hand – is a unique feat in itself, and this Mr. Nast accomplishes with astonishing rapidity and ease. He produces his best effects by bold strokes, few in number, but all telling and to the point. A striking instance of this is his conversion of a rough and ready portrait of President Roosevelt into an instantly recognizable likeness of the Rev. Charles H. Parkhurst of New York "Reform" renown. Mr. Nast has acquired the actor art of getting on visitor terms with his public, and his turn has come to be regarded as one of the happiest and daintiest of recent outgivings in the constantly changing world … and the novelty as well as its cleverness drew great applause for the artist … an accomplishment that no one else has achieved; Tribune – His work is wonderful, rapid, entertaining; Journal - … displayed remarkable cleverness in rapid caricatures with the crayon, working with both hands, each producing a separate likeness. Saginaw, Mich: Courier Herald – Thomas Nast Jr., the ambidextrous caricaturist, did splendidly last night … The production was beautiful and brought out exclamations from the audience; Evening News – An unusually interesting feature is the work of Thomas Nast Jr., a caricaturist that works with both hands, and actually draws two heads at one and the same time, differing in feature and expression and quite typical of the people they represent. St. Louis: Globe Democrat – Thomas Nast Jr., "ambidextrous caricaturist" is a wonder. He draws bold familiar types, one with each hand, completing both at the same time; Post Dispatch – Thomas Nast Jr., son of the father, and most proficient of ambidextrous artists … His work is of a high order and is instructive as well as most entertaining.*

Page 4 is pictorial in nature. Since Mr. Nast Sr. died in Dec 1902, and Thomas Jr. does a remembrance portion of his act for his late father, the dates of 1901 and 1902 on the playbill are confusing.

One very interesting item I discovered about Thomas Jr. is that he created a stained glass window for his sister Mabel Crawford's home in New Rochelle, New York in 1902. The picture is of Father Christmas holding the Christ Child, titled 'Christmas Eve'.

I cannot find Thomas Jr. on the 1910 census in any of the several databases I use.

On the 1920 Mamaroneck, Westchester, New York census Thomas Jr., age 54, and Ella B., age 53 are living in a house they own with a mortgage. He is an artist who works at home. Ella was born in New York as was her mother. Her father was born in England. Thomas Jr. and Ella have no children.

Ella died on 27 Aug 1924 in Larchmont, Westchester, New York.

On the 1930 New Rochelle, Westchester, New York census Thomas Jr. is living in the household of his brother Cyril at age 65. He is a widower. Cyril is 50 and his wife Marie S. is 53. Cyril and Marie's son Thomas is 15. Their home is valued at $35,000. They own a radio. Cyril is the advertising manager of an electric company and Thomas Jr. has no occupation.

I have not found a death record for Thomas Jr. or where he is buried. The Social Security Death Index came up with nothing. He was listed as a survivor on his mother, Sarah Nast's obituary in 1932. On a 1936 New Rochelle city directory, Thomas Jr. is no longer living in his brother Cyril's household. This of course does not mean he exited Cyril's home through death. It will be interesting to see if he is on the upcoming 1940 Federal census that comes out in April.

Edith Nast

Sarah Edith Nast married Robert H. E. Porter 26 Sep 1891 in Morristown, New Jersey. They were both born in 1868 and were 23 years old when they married. Robert's parents were General Fritz John Porter and Harriet P. Cook Porter. On the 1885 Morris County, New Jersey census, Robert has siblings Lucia C., Evalina S., Holbrook F. J. There are three non family members in the household, probably servants.

Robert H., age 12, is on the 1880 Morristown census in the household of his father Fitz John Porter. He was born in New Jersey; however, his older siblings were born in New York. The Porter home was Dwelling 45 Family 107. The Nast home was Dwelling 285 and Family 347. Both are beautiful historic mansions in Morristown, New Jersey. You can find pictures of both online.

On 22 Feb 1893, Edith gave birth to a son who died the same day, un named, Male Porter.

On 14 Mar 1894 Edith gave birth to a son as yet unnamed, Male Porter.

I have not found Robert and Edith on the 1900 census. Robert Porter is mentioned in 1899 articles about his sister-in-law Julia Nast's death, along with her brother, Thomas Nast Jr., as arranging for the removal of her body to a mortuary after her untimely demise.

Sarah Edith Porter filed for divorce from her husband Robert H. E. Porter in Jan 1906. The grounds that were filed were desertion and non support. After their marriage, they lived in Pittsburg, Pennsylvania where Robert was connected to one of the large steel industries. Edith states she has not seen Robert since July of 1903 and has supported herself and her son as a nurse at Presbyterian Hospital, New York, and has made her home with her mother and brother Cyril at Morristown. She, her family, and her lawyer have failed to locate Robert in spite of an exhaustive search. It is interesting to note that Robert's brother Holbrook Fitz John Porter is on a Pennsylvania census in 1900 but Robert, Edith and Thomas N. are not living with him. They are also not living with any other of their relatives that I can find. Many census records are too faded to be decipherable or the bottom is so blackened nothing shows through.

Edith's first husband, Robert H. E. Porter, the father of her son, was the son of a military hero, a man of means with servants to care for his family's home, as was the Nast family. Robert's father, General Fitz John Porter was born in Portsmouth, Rockingham, New Hampshire 31 Aug 1822. He married Harriet Pierson Cook 19 Mar 1857.

Edith Porter married Ralph Woodford St. Hill 27 Apr 1907 in Manhattan, New York. Ralph's father was Harry S. St. Hill and his mother was Mary Tuscan. It is possible that Edith's son was adopted by Ralph St. Hill before her death in 1909, but whether Thomas made a personal chose to take Mr. St. Hill's name or actually had it changed legally is a personal preference and has nothing to do with genealogy. His descendants have access to some very valuable bloodline information in an easy online search. Major General Fitz John Porter was a Civil War hero unjustly court marshaled by political rivals and later his good name was restored. There are some incredible pictures of him in the Civil War on the Library of Congress Web site. There is also a huge monument of General Porter sitting on a horse in Portsmouth, New Hampshire. The Porters, one of the strongest military families in the nation's history, represented a long distinguished line of military service.

Edith Nast Porter St. Hill died 4 Aug 1909 in Manhattan. She was 35. She is buried in Woodlawn Cemetery in the Bronx in section South 12054 owned by Ralph St. Hill.

Ralph is listed on the 1910 census in the home of his mother-in-law Sarah Nast, the details of which are described under the section relating to Mrs. Nast.

Ralph St. Hill, age 26, appeared on the 1900 Shandaken Township Ulster New York census, born 1874 in New Zealand, single and head of household. His father was born in the West Indies and his mother in England. Ralph migrated to the U.S. in 1899. A woman was living with him named Delia Frisbie, age 21, and was listed as a boarder with an occupation of servant. Ralph is an author. Neither of them has a child, and if a child did result from a union between the two, it would not match the child living in the household of Sarah Nast in 1910 as her grandchild.

Ralph W. St. Hill co-founded a business called Truth Well Told, an advertising agency of which his brother-in-law Thomas Nast Jr. was the agency's first art director. Ralph designed the logo Truth Well Told for the company and Thomas Jr. developed the figure, chiseling the slogan Truth Well Told from solid rock.

Mabel Nast

Mabel is on the 1880 census in the household of her parents, age 8.

I have not found a marriage record for Mabel.

On 10 May 1893 Mabel and John William R. Crawford had a baby girl in Morristown, New Jersey. John was 26 and Mabel was 22. The baby was un named but later census records reveal the child was Muriel.

On 26 Mar 1895 John and Mabel had a son in Essex County, New Jersey. He was un named but census records later reveal his identity as John W, Jr.

On 27 Sep 1897 Mabel and John had a son in Middlesex County, New Jersey, Thomas N. Crawford. John was 30 and Mabel was 26.

On the 1900 Middlesex, New Jersey census Mable and John have been married seven years, have three children all of whom are living, Muriel, John W. and Thomas M [sic]. There are two servants Daisy M. Martin and Lillian Martin.

On the 1910 Brooklyn, Kings County, New York census, John W. R. Crawford is 42, Mabel N. is 38, Muriel N. is 15, John W. R. is 14, Thomas N. is 12, and two servants live with the family, Olive J. Hueston 25, and Venita M. Joseph 30.

On the 1920 Westchester, New York census Mabel was 48, her husband John W. Crawford was 52, their son John W. was 23, son Thomas M 22, Muriel (Crawford) Batty 25 years, her husband, Donald Batty 30, Muriel Batty, 3 years six months, Donald Batty, 1 year seven months.

On the 1930 New Rochelle, Westchester, New York census John is 58, Mabel is 54, and Sarah Nast is 88. There are three servants.

Muriel Nast Crawford was married in Sep 1915 to Donald Ellerby Batty, son of Mr/Mrs William J. Batty, at her parent's home in New Rochelle, New York. Ushers were her brothers and a cousin, Thomas Nast St. Hill.

Mabel Nast Crawford was on a passenger list from Liverpool to New York in 1913.

Mabel Nast Crawford died 12 Dec 1965 in New Rochelle, New York. Her husband, John William Roy Crawford, preceded her in death 6 Jul 1939, age 71.

Cyril Nast

Cyril is on the 1895 New Jersey State census in the home of his parents in Morristown; the 1900 U.S. Federal census in Morristown with his parents; on the 1910 Federal census in Brooklyn, Kings, New York in the home of his mother Sarah; and on the 1920 Federal census in New Rochelle, Westchester, New York as head of household and his mother Sarah is living with him and his family. In 1930 Cyril, age 50, is head of household on the New Rochelle census living with wife Marie S. 53 and son Thomas 15. His bother Thomas Jr., 65, lives with the family.

On 12 Sep 1910, Cyril, age 31, departed Kingston, Jamaica on the ship S. S. Albingia destination New York City.

Cyril and Marie Annette Serre were married in Manhattan on 12 Nov 1910 at her home. He lived with his mother Sarah at 51 Quincy St. in Manhattan. His sister Mabel Crawford lived at 357 Washington Ave in Brooklyn. It would be interesting to see if these building are still standing and what they look like today.

Cyril registered for the draft at age 39 on 12 Sep 1918. He listed his birth date as 28 Aug 1879. His occupation was advertising manager. He was married to Marie S. They live in New Rochelle, New York. His signature is interesting and I wish it was clearer. The bottom of the C is extended in a line to the right, with the rest of the letters of the first name, 'yril', written on that line, exactly like I write my name Christine. Most of the draft card is illegible. It looks as if under 'height' Cyril is listed as being tall and under 'build' he is listed as being slender. His eyes were brown and the color of his hair was either black or blond. There were no disabling features on his body.

Cyril was an accomplished tennis player who was one of the winners of the first round singles match in an annual tournament at the Quail Ridge New Rochelle Tennis Club championship, June, 1921.

Cyril is mentioned in his mother Sarah Nast's obituary and death notice in 1932 and his wife Marie's obituary; she died 25 Jul 1954 at age 77.

He is mentioned in his sister Mabel Nast Crawford's obituary. She died 12 Dec 1965. Her husband is noted as having died before her. She is survived by her brother Cyril and seven grandchildren. This would imply her brother Thomas Jr. preceded in death so while it is a huge time span, Thomas Jr. died between 1932 and 1965. It is interesting that Cyril died a year after his sister Mabel.

Cyril and his grandson Thomas Nast Jr. share a stone in Woodlawn Cemetery in the Bronx. It reads Cyril Nast 1879 – 1966 and Thomas Nast Jr. 1942 – 1997. Thomas Nast Jr. was the son of Cyril's son Thomas Nast, who is also interred at Woodlawn cemetery in the Bronx.

All of Mr. Nast's children who had children named them after him; what a glowing tribute to the man their father was.

Thomas Nast 1859

© Christine Hayes

Miss Sarah Edwards

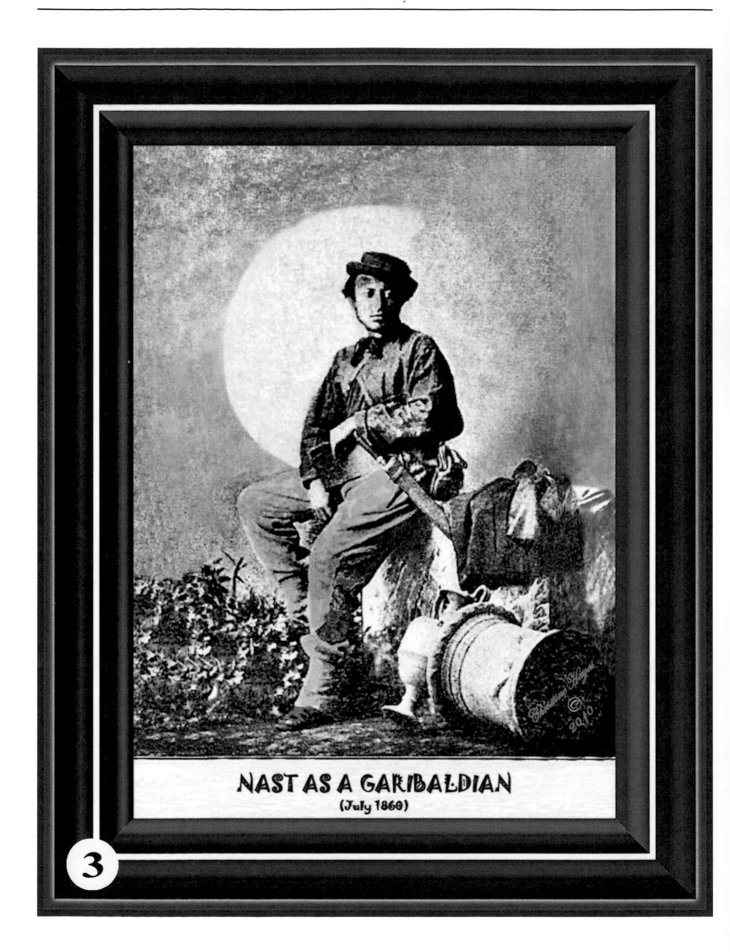

NAST AS A GARIBALDIAN
(July 1860)

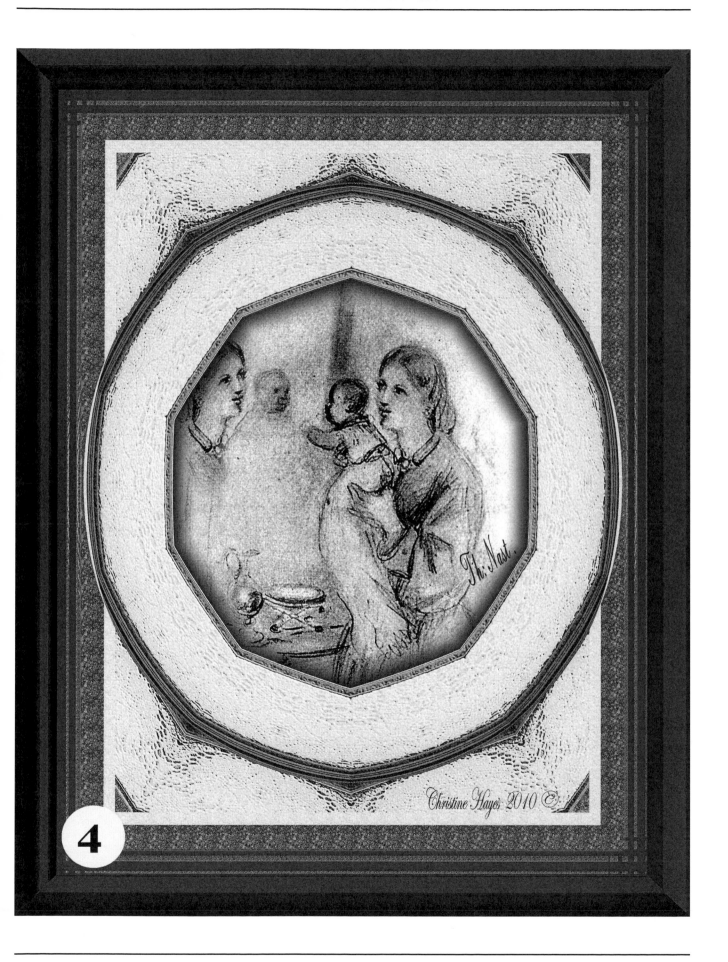

THOMAS NAST 1877

Thomas Nast - An Early Self Portrait *Christine Hayes © 2010*

7

Christine Hayes © 2010

THOMAS NAST

8

Thomas Nast

Christine Hayes © 2010

9

Christine Hayes ©2010

Appolonia Abriss Nast · Original Sketch by Son Thomas Nast

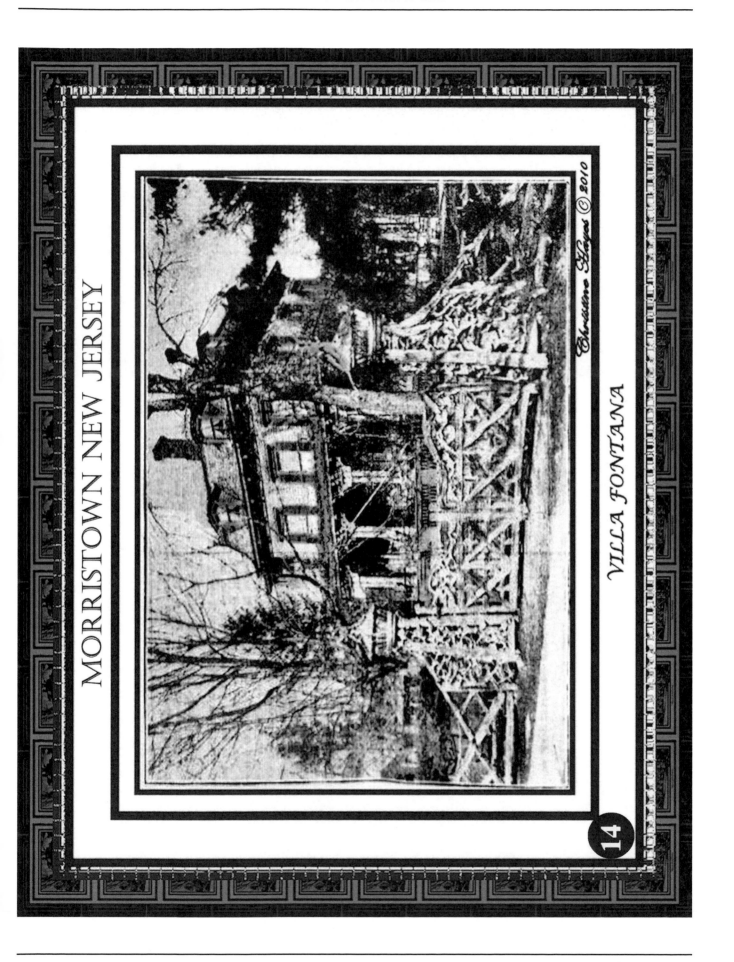

MORRISTOWN NEW JERSEY

VILLA FONTANA

14

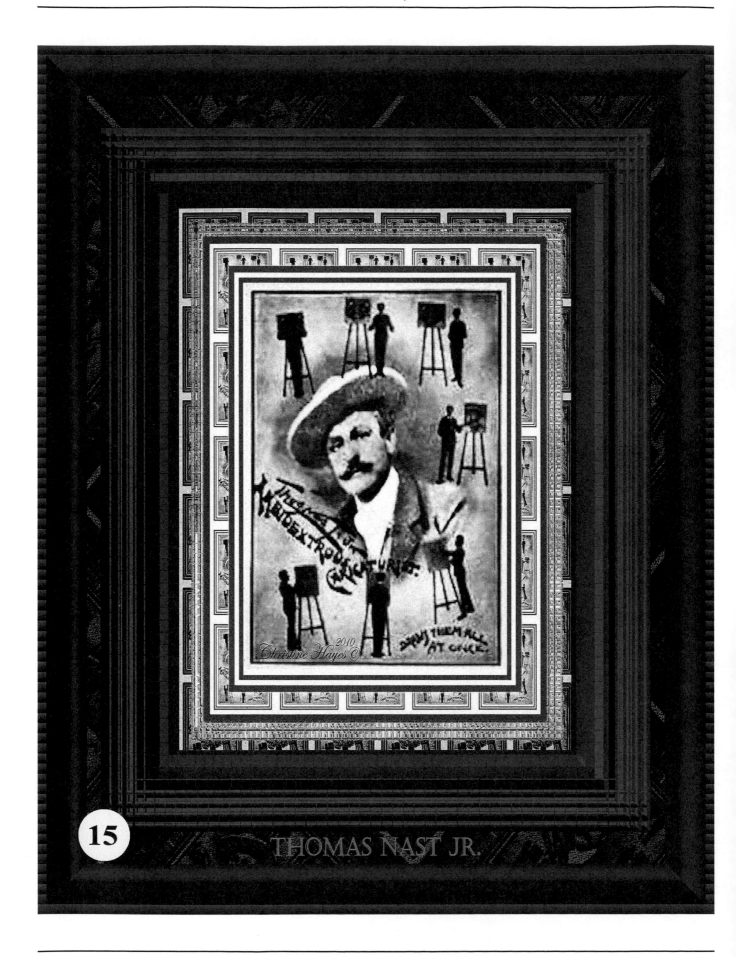

Mabel & Cyril 1880

16

Christine Hayes © 2010

17 *Mr. Nast Painting Lee Awaiting Grant*

Nast Family

America

Germany

Joannis Busch
Joannae ?
Joannis Nicolai Gerracht
Annae Apolloniae Schardein

George Abriss
Anna Catharina Rapp
Andreas Busch
Eva Catharina Gerracht

Pauli Nast
Josephi Thomae Nast
Catharina Walbrunn

Joanne Georgio Michaele Abriss
Josephus Christophorus Abriss
Maria Catharina Bushin

Frank Christoph Vogt
Eva Catharina Vogtin
Elizabetha ?

Apollonia Abriss

Thomas Nast

18

The Art of Thomas Nast

Brief Descriptions of the Illustrations As They Appear In Order at the End of This Section

1. OUR FLAG 1864

This was the first image I sketched and hand painted. I particularly love this picture of Lady Liberty and our flag. I used the colors 'of the time' which weren't quite the red and blue in patriotic pictures of today. You can find Civil War images online that show the colors used then or get some books about uniforms at the library. I used very small brushes for the tiny detail, the largest being a #6 flat but primarily using #4 and #2. I clipped an old brush with scissors down to just a couple of hairs for some of the finer work. I used acrylic paint thinned with an extender. One could also use oil thinned with odorless turpentine but it involves more clean up and dry time. I used a foam plate for the tiny dots of paint necessary and mixed the paint right on the plate, then discarded it after use. I used only one paper towel in completing this painting. It is amazing how the blacks, whites, and grays show through the thin transparent layer of paint to look like a real painting, and it requires no artistic talent at all. There are different kinds of paper at arts and crafts stores on which you can print your picture, such as canvas paper and actual sheets of canvas that I use in my printer. Once you put your picture behind glass in a ready made portrait frame complete with an 8X10 opening, you have an incredibly beautiful and professional looking painting.

There are expensive apparatuses on the market to render a duplicate sketch if you need to do that. One of these apparatuses is called a tracing projector, and another is called a pantograph which is great for enlarging images. Just as effective and cost free is a grid method of ten horizontal and ten vertical lines on a copy of the picture, and repeating the same grid on a sheet of card stock. Shade in the squares exactly as they appear on the picture and it will create a very good duplication of the image. Be aware these old pictures have darkened areas where the pages met if they were a double page image and make allowances for that in your sketch, otherwise, those same dark fold areas will be in your finished project. I did not realize this when I first did the drawing of Our Flag and I then had to repair it. It is easier to make allowances for those center folds at the time you are sketching them than to rework it after the fact. Once your sketch is finished, before painting, you must either scan it into your computer and print it on card stock, or, spray your sketch with fixative to keep the pencil lead from smearing.

I left out areas of most of the sketches that I re drew and added flowers and other embellishments to some. On this picture of the flag, I emphasized the mountains in the background and added a moon.

This is a quick, easy, effective way to paint black and white family photos as well as art work.

2. CHRISTMAS EVE/LAST SLEEP 1862

This scene depicts a union soldier looking at a letter or pictures from his family and in another vignette his wife is praying for him as their children lie sleeping in bed. This poignant scene is further saddened by the mounds of graves in the foreground, a grim reminder of what the possibilities for the soldier and his wife and children were. Out of all the Civil War drawings by Mr. Nast, this one had to be the most popular, bringing tears to grown men's eyes, especially military men or loved ones of those who served. This is the drawing that piqued my original interest in Mr. Nast's work because it poignantly reminded me of the book Last Sleep, the Battle of Droop Mountain by West Virginia Historian Terry Lowry.

In a letter of reply to a man who wanted to buy his Civil War sketches, Mr. Nast disclosed how very much they meant to him. Note this letter was written less than four months after Mr. Nast's first child, Julia, had died.

Morristown, N.J.
August 24, 1899
Mr. Robert Carter,

Dear Sir
I think that the Civil War sketches and portraits that I have are more valuable to me than to you. But if you come to New York sometimes, I might meet with you and talk it over, or if you ever visit Morristown, I could show you what I have. I was away when your letter came, hence the delay in replying.

Yours Truly, **Th: Nast.**

3. AFTER ALL 1881

Mr. Nast drew this picture as a remembrance of President James A. Garfield who died on 19 Sep 1881 from the wounds inflicted by an assassin. This image has been recreated by many artists in many different artistic expressions. My own beautiful garden statue of this image to which the sculptor added angel wings is displayed in my picture on the back of the book. Mr. Nast also used this same pose in Illustration 7 "Compromise With the South" showing Columbia kneeling over a grave.

4. SAINT VALENTINE'S DAY 1861

I have seen this sketch offered for sale on both E-Bay and private Internet sites, and Mr. Nast is not given credit as the artist. This was quite disturbing to me. One such site listed their public domain acquisition as the Library of Congress, and thus I went to the Library of Congress Web site and they did not acknowledge Mr. Nast as the artist either. Indeed, this is one of my favorite pieces of artistic brilliance by Mr. Nast but I think credit must be given where credit is due and thus I include this beautiful image here. I am certain the seated woman is Sarah Edwards reading a letter from Mr. Nast when he was following Garibaldie in Italy, and the one standing behind her is probably one of her sisters.

5. A GALLANT COLOR BEARER Sep 1862

H. Alexander, the color-bearer of the 10th New York Regiment, clinging to American flag, after receiving three wounds.

6. AND NOT THIS MAN? 1865

This picture was the compliment to another image on the left showing Lee and others kneeling before Columbia and she is asking, "Shall I trust these men?"

7. COMPROMISE WITH the SOUTH Sep 1864

I actually drew an almost identical image kneeling over a grave in a poem about Mountaintop Removal Surface Mining in West Virginia. It was quite an eerie feeling.

8. THE HERO OF OUR AGE DEAD Aug 1885

Mr. Nast loved and respected President Grant.

9. THANKS TO GRANT w/ COLUMBIA Chicago May 1868

10. GRANT, WASHINGTON, and LINCOLN – 1875

Say not thou, "What is the cause that the former days were better than these? For thou dost not inquire wisely concerning this." – Solomon

Mr. Nast's son, Thos: Jr., said he thought Mr. Nast belonged up there with Grant, Washington, and Lincoln; I wholeheartedly agree.

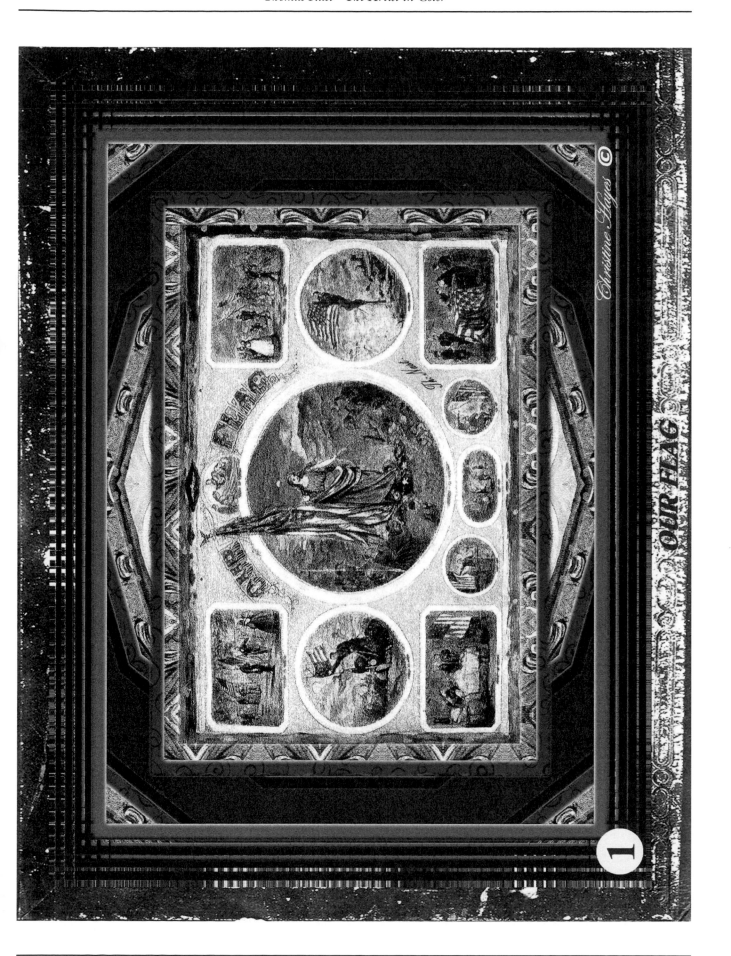

A Gallant Color Bearer

Christine Hayes 2010 ©

AND NOT THIS MAN

6   *And Not This Man?*

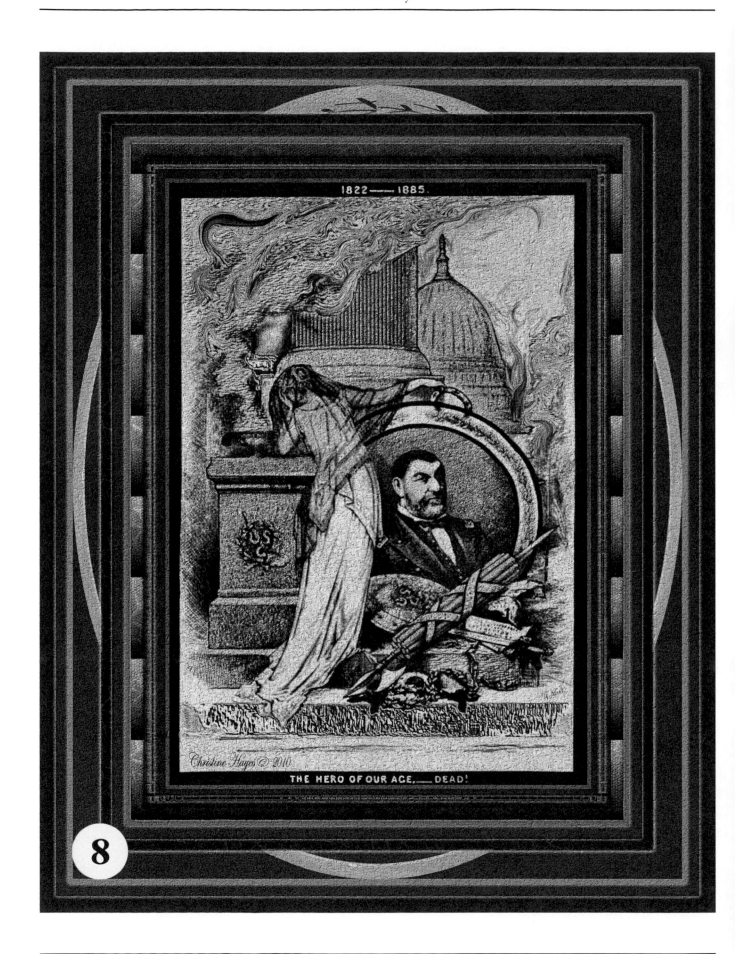

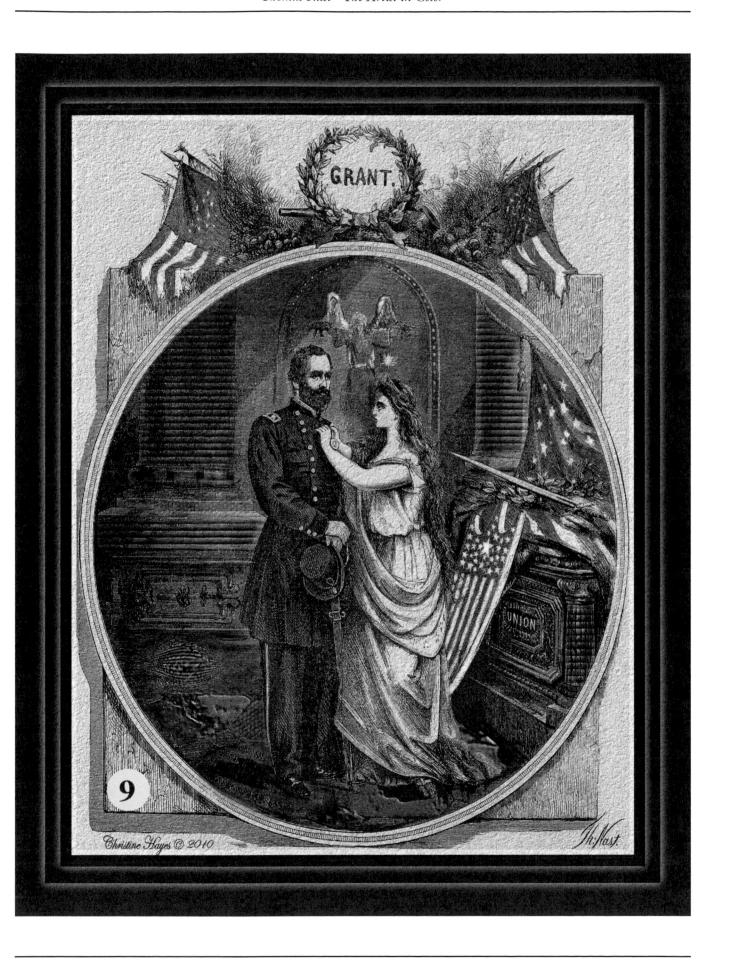

The POLITICAL STATEMENTS of THOMAS NAST

To understand the political atmosphere throughout Europe's history requires looking outside the American perspective. Europeans know their history, and fear it rearing its head again and again. Americans look at European events in history through the prism of freedom and democracy. They do not understand Socialism; that it has two heads, a leftwing Communist agenda like the old Soviet Union, and a rightwing Nazi Socialism, or National Capitalism like in Germany. Most Americans, if asked whether Hitler was left or rightwing would say rightwing but they would assume he was a Conservative because Americans associate violence and extreme rhetoric with rightwing Conservatives, but they would be wrong. The European masses have been caught in, and between, these two political ideologies of Socialism over hundreds of years, to the tune of massive death and destruction unlike anywhere else on earth. Napoleon was responsible for 2.5 million deaths during his reign as emperor of France in conflicts involving every major European power from 1804 to 1815, and this would have been in the recent memories of Mr. Nast parents, his mother being born in 1801 and his father near that time.

Americans also do not know the history of the two predominant European/Asian religions, Catholic and Islam, at war with each other since the Crusades. Charlemagne and the First Reich killed over 50 million people if they did not convert to Catholicism. Again, the skewed American perspective about these religions is colored by the religious tolerance by Americans. But Thomas Nast lived in the middle of this chaos, and no doubt had heard the horror stories handed down by parents and grandparents of what can happen in a Church/State governing body, whether leftwing or rightwing Socialists. Mr. Nast hated Socialists so it is ludicrous for anyone to deduce that his father was a Socialist. He also hated the union of church and state because he knew what it could, and would, do if it ever caught hold in America. Mr. Nast held a deep love for this country and he was fiercely loyal to America. He proudly wore his patriotism on his sleeve. He was neither Republican as has been reported, nor Democrat; rather a patriot in solid support of what was best for the nation, putting the country above political parties as evidenced by Illustration 2 "Party Whip". He held neither a left nor right wing agenda; rather his truth had no agenda and he stood for truth and common sense. He has been accused of prejudice against Catholics and Irish which is absurdly untrue; look to his blackboard for the evidence this was not the case. In illustration 4 he makes it clear he sees a great threat to America by the union of church and state and in illustration 11 he shows compassion for the plight of the Irish. Further, he had servants who were born in Ireland and were a part of his home. What Mr. Nast most assuredly did not like was crime, corruption, and cronyism such as the Hibernian Riots in New York City in 1870/71 during which Tammany Hall employed Irish thugs to attack innocent citizens, killing some and injuring others including women and children. A consistent and recurring theme of reverence and respect for women and children runs through all of Mr. Nast work.

Mr. Nast centrist position in full support and defense of the nation against any who might dare bring tyranny and anarchy to its shores is one of the ways that he was like the television and radio commentator, Glenn Beck. Mr. Beck also reflects Thomas Nast's lecture method by his famous blackboard. In an interview by a Chicago Times reporter, Mr. Nast had lost his voice from lecturing, but this did not stop him from responding to the reporter. He brought out a large blackboard from under the bed in his hotel room and using a crayon, commenced to draw pictures in answer to the reporter's questions. The blackboard was used at lectures Mr. Nast held all over the country. We Americans are at a crucial point in our history; we are under the delusion that the goose that laid the golden egg will never run out of eggs, that America cannot fail, much like Mr. Nast portrayed in Illustration 9 at the end of this section. Mr. Nast's message of 150 years ago is the same message that television and radio commentator Glenn Beck espouses today. It is almost as if Mr. Nast is giving it one last ditch effort to save the nation. Let us all pray that he is successful because our children's future depends on it.

When setting sail for Ecuador, he waved a little handkerchief of the Stars and Stripes to his friends and family seeing him off on the pier. Sadly, he would not return.

We can all learn a lesson studying Thomas Nast and looking honestly at ourselves individually; at the many factions of our society realistically: and at our political parties, religious movements, social programs, media outlets, financial institutions, and business models with objective critical thinking without bias. We Americans are a great peoples who have been reared to be tolerant, generous, and forgiving; that is a good thing that can snare us into complacency about unscrupulous persons and groups that take advantage of our open, free, and tolerant views. I wonder what Mr. Nast would say about the rapacious plunder and civic shame that stalks the halls of political ambition today.

The eleven following images are indicative of our present day social and political ills in the United States. One can only imagine what Mr. Nast would say about illegal 'immigration', political correctness, the national debt, corrupt politicians and corporate America, the banking scandal, our weakened military, our overflowing prisons, and foreign policy. You can be assured of one thing; he would not make excuses for people taking advantage of and abusing the law and order of the nation.

1. LIBERTY IS NOT ANARCHY 1886

Our nation has become so politically correct in today's social, political, and media environment that we are not allowed to give an honest and truthful review of anyone or any group of color.

2. PARTY WHIP

The End Of Party Slavery 1885

Party Slave Driver: "If we can't whip these Mugwumps into shape, our occupation will be gone."

While Mr. Nast did vote Republican most of the time, he did not identify himself as a 'Republican', rather, he identified himself as an American who did the best thing he could do for the good of the country regardless of personal agenda. He knew the dangers of putting 'Party' above 'National Good', and as we can see in today's America, party worship has divided our country and made us vulnerable. Both parties are against whatever the other party does even if they know it is in the best interest of the country, and both parties are only interested in getting re elected. Mr. Nast was against putting 'Party' above 'Country', without respect to either party.

3. IMMIGRANTS

REFORM IS NECESSARY IN THE FOREIGN LINE 1877

The U.S. (Like an uncle) "If you come simply as Americans, this is the place. But if you persist in your distinct nationality, you must call at the State Department where all foreign affairs are considered."

As you can see, Mr. Nast included both German and Irish immigrants in image 3.

4. CHURCH & STATE

A Legitimate Question About Home Rule Mar 1875

U.S. Republic: "To whom do you owe your first allegiance?"

Hon. F. Kernan (From New York [?] "This is a very embarrassing position to be placed in."

5. CHANGE

Women Will Never Be Statesmen - Oct 1880

Pat. "Where's the dinner?"

Wife. "Ah! Since ye've had stiddy wurrk, haven't ye had splendid dinners! And now yer always talking about change, change, change, and sure I thought I'd give ye wan."

6. THE BANKING CRISIS

A Financial Lesson Aug – 1876

An eagle stayed his flight and entreated a lion to make an alliance with him to their mutual advantage. The lion replied, "I have no objection, but you must excuse me for requiring you to find surety for your good faith, for how can I trust anyone as a friend who is able to fly away from his bargain whenever he pleases?" Aesop

7. THE NATIONAL DEBT

Ideal Money - Jan 1878

"Universal Suffrage can, if it likes, repudiate the whole debt; it can, if it likes, decree soft-soap to be currency." – The Louieville Courier-Journal

Our treasury is printing money today that is not backed by gold; in other words, we are buying our own I.O.U.s with an I.O.U.

8. INFLATION

By Inflation You Will Burst – 1873

Prices are rising dramatically even as I write this. With turmoil in the Middle East, and the future of oil transports in question, considering oil is used for almost everything we buy, inflation is almost certain.

9. SPENDING – WE CAN'T GO BROKE

Always Killing the Goose That Lays the Golden Egg 1878

Communist Statesman (without responsibility) "Nothing in it, after all; it's too bad; now I thought he was just full of them."

10. OUR MILITARY

There Is Nothing Mean About Us 1874

Uncle Sam: "What Congress proposes to reduce our military to."

As Mr. Nast's picture shows, we are reducing our military to Skin and Bones.

11. The Irish

The Herald of relief from America - We are starving Ireland 1880

This picture, showing an Irish woman pleading for help from an American ship, with her people starving behind her, as well as Illustration 3 about immigrants in which Mr. Nast puts the German people on Uncle Sam's left and the Irish on the right without regard to one or the other, disproves the statements that he was prejudiced against the Irish. Mr. Nast was against lawlessness, corruption, and disloyalty in any form, but he was never against the Irish people.

THE END OF PARTY SLAVERY

PARTY SLAVE DRIVER. "If we can't whip these Mugwumps into shape, our occupation will be gone."

Oct 1885

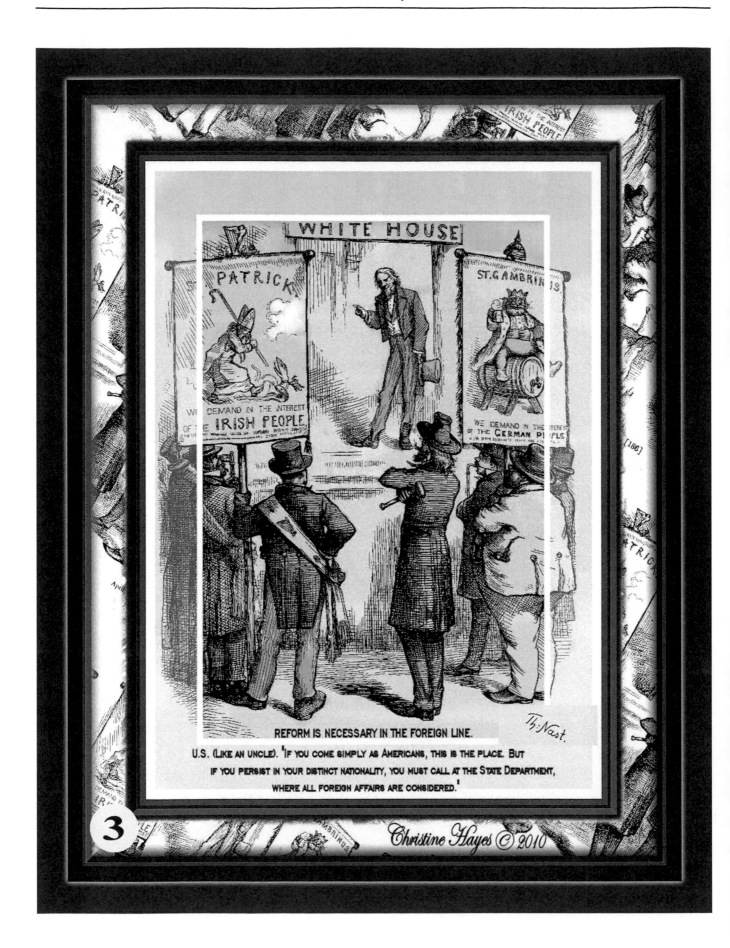

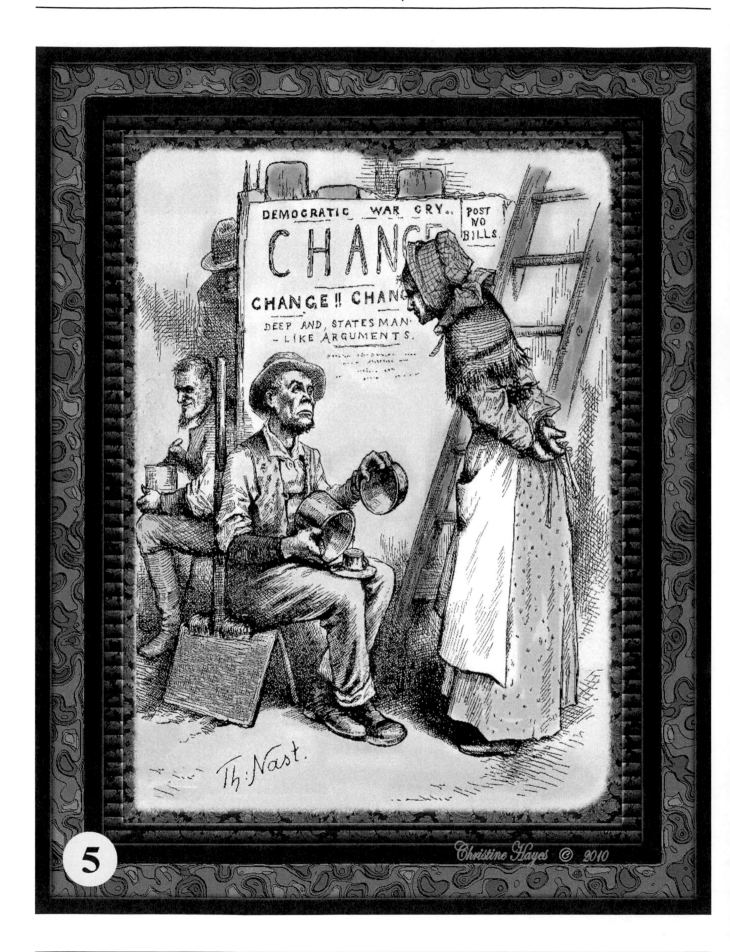

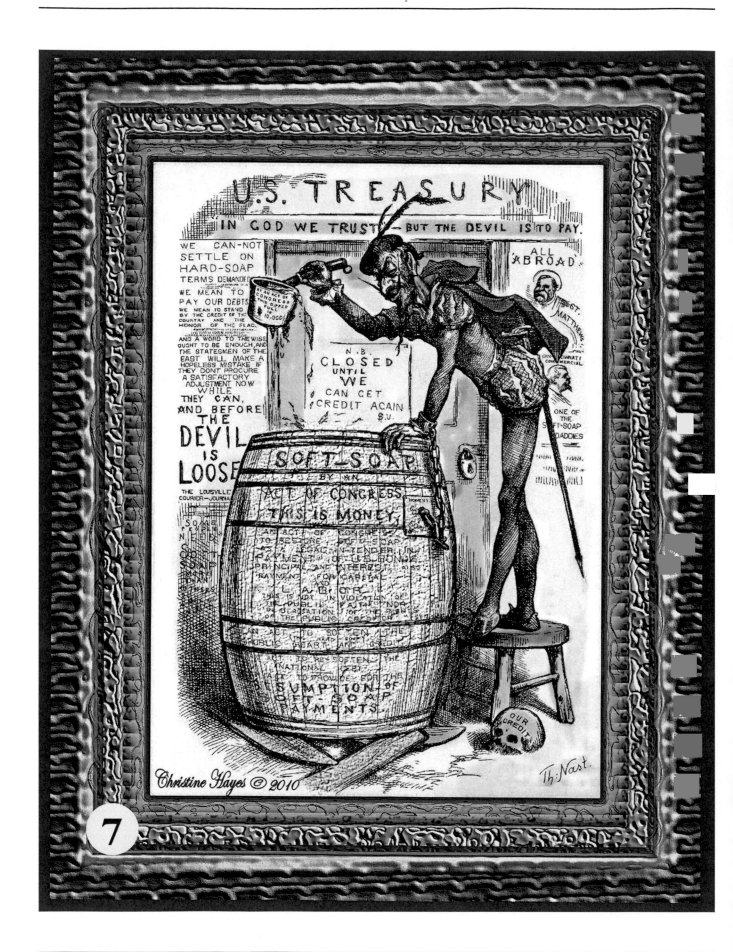

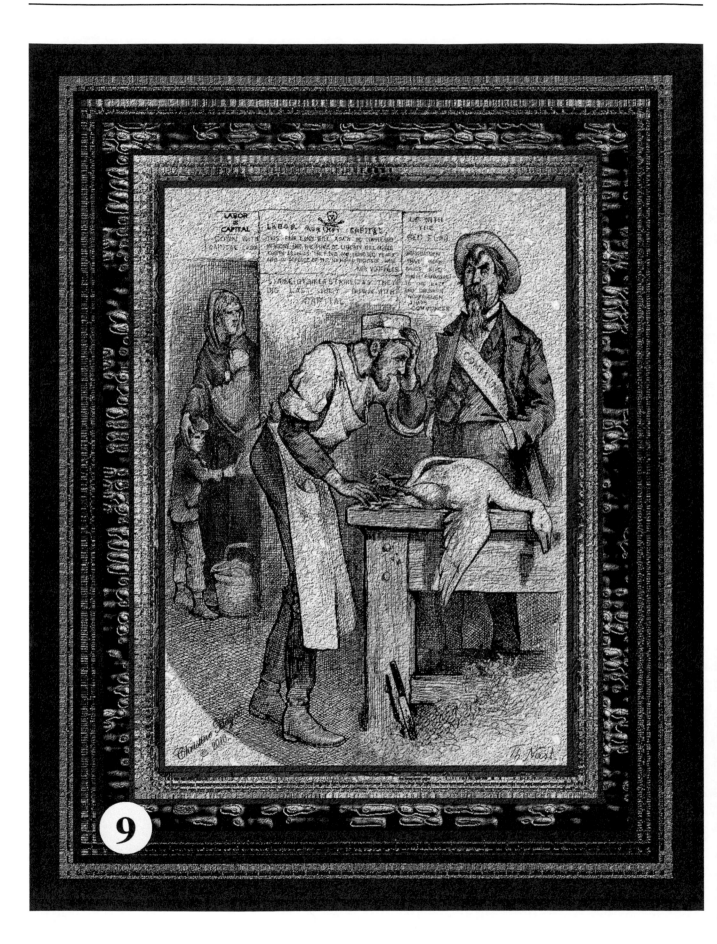

The End

Printed by Publishers' Graphics LLC
PGD-05416